THEOLOGY

THE
BASICS

"This book is ecumenical in the best sense of that word. McGrath appeals to the breadth and depth of the Church's witness in order to explain its faith, and in so doing he has produced a superb guidebook for the study of theology. The book should engage students of all stripes. It raises as many questions as it answers, and it provides the foundation for a deeper exploration of the Church's common mind."

Mark Weedman, Crossroads College

"At one point, Professor McGrath aptly describes this book as a handshake of welcome for those who want to begin the study of Christian theology. Written in a style that is friendly, clear, and accessible, it inducts the novice into a masterly overview of the subject and into the lively, questioning conversation that it represents."

Jeremy Worthen, South East Institute for Theological Education and University of Kent

"What makes this book such an effective introduction to the essential ingredients of the Christian faith is the way in which Alister McGrath interweaves leading theological ideas with the views of major theologians. The result is a compact but thorough volume that is sound, useful, and remarkably appealing. Highly recommended as a basic text for both beginning and intermediate classes in Christian theology."

David Hein, Hood College Maryland

"McGrath has successfully created a theology which is both inviting to the beginning student and informing to the more advanced student. His approach often offers a unique perspective on how to warmly introduce a student to complex discussions on theology. This book will be useful on many levels in the Church and the academy as an introductory theology."

David Talley, Talbot School of Theology, Biola University

THEOLOGY

THE
BASICS

ALISTER E. McGRATH

Blackwell
Publishing

BLACKWELL PUBLISHING
350 Main Street, Malden, MA 02148-5020, USA
9600 Garsington Road, Oxford OX4 2DQ, UK
550 Swanston Street, Carlton, Victoria 3053, Australia

The right of Alister E. McGrath to be identified as the Author of this Work has been asserted in accordance with the UK Copyright, Designs, and Patents Act 1988.

First published 2004 by Blackwell Publishing Ltd

4   2005

Library of Congress Cataloging-in-Publication Data

McGrath, Alister E., 1953-
  Theology : the basics / Alister E. McGrath.
    p. cm.
  Includes bibliographical references and index.
  ISBN 1-4051-1424-X (alk. paper)–ISBN 1-4051-1425-8 (pbk.: alk. paper)
  1. Theology, Doctrinal–Popular works. I. Title.

BT77.M382 2004
230–dc22

                                                            2003022140

ISBN-13: 978-1-4051-1424-0 (alk. paper)–ISBN-13: 978-1-4051-1425-7 (pbk.: alk. paper)

A catalogue record for this title is available from the British Library.

Set in 10.5 on 13pt Galliard
by Kolam Information Services Pvt. Ltd, Pondicherry, India
Printed and bound in the United Kingdom
by TJ International, Padstow, Cornwall

The publisher's policy is to use permanent paper from mills that operate a sustainable forestry policy, and which has been manufactured from pulp processed using acid-free and elementary chlorine-free practices. Furthermore, the publisher ensures that the text paper and cover board used have met acceptable environmental accreditation standards.

For further information on
Blackwell Publishing, visit our website:
www.blackwellpublishing.com

Contents

Preface

What is theology? The word has been used by Christians since the third century to mean "talking about God." "Christian theology" thus means something like "talking about God in a Christian way," recognizing that the word "god" means quite different things to different religious traditions. Christians think about their faith; "theology" is the term used for this process of reflection, and its outcome. To study theology, therefore, is to think systematically about the fundamental ideas of Christianity. It is intellectual reflection on the act, content, and implications of the Christian faith.

Sometimes this means deciding what is the best way of understanding some aspect of the Christian faith. A good example is provided by the doctrine of the church. For some, the church is a "mixed body," consisting of believers and unbelievers; for others, it is a "pure body," consisting only of believers. Other examples can easily be given. So where do these different approaches come from? What are their merits and their implications? What difference do they make to the business of Christian living?

At other times, theological reflection means trying to under-stand why the Christian churches committed themselves to ideas which, at least at first sight, seem complicated and even a little implausible. Why should Christians believe that Jesus Christ is "truly divine and truly human," when this seems much more difficult than a simpler statement such as "Jesus Christ is truly human"? Or, to take another familiar example, why should anyone want to believe that God is a Trinity – "one God, three persons" – when this seems so much more complicated than simply believing in God?

There are many reasons for wanting to think about the Chris-tian faith in more detail. Those who are not Christians will be interested in learning what Christians believe, and why. Theology offers an explanation of the Christian faith, and helps us to see why Christians differ on certain points of importance. At the very least, a basic understanding of Christian theology will be invalu-able to anyone studying Western cultural history, literature, or art.

In the case of Christians, theological reflection can lead to personal enrichment, and a deepened appreciation of their faith. For the great Christian theologian Augustine of Hippo, there is a genuine intellectual excitement in "wrestling with God." He spoke of an "*eros* of the mind" – a sense of longing to understand more about God's nature and ways – and the transforming impact that this could have on people's lives. Other Christian writers have stressed the practical importance of theology, noting how it is essential for the ministry of the church. Preaching, spirituality, and pastoral care, many argue, are ultimately grounded in theology. This business of "thinking about God" takes place at many levels – in church study groups, in Bible studies, through preaching, and in academic seminars.

This short, basic introduction to Christian theology is aimed specifically at those who are approaching it for the first time, and who feel intimidated by the thought of studying theology. The book sets out to introduce you to some of Christian theology's basic themes, problems, and personalities, and to whet your appetite to know more. There are severe limits to what can be dealt with in such a short book, and many readers will find themselves frustrated by the brevity of some discussions. Happily, there are plenty of other works that will be able to take your studies further. This book will make specific suggestions about what you can do next, once you have finished this introduction.

The book sets out to explore some of the basic ideas of Christianity, engaging with some of its leading representatives. It *aims* to introduce you to the basics of Christian theology. It *assumes* that you know nothing about the subject. It *introduces and explains* the following aspects of Christian theology:

- some of its leading ideas, as they are found in the Apostles' Creed;
- how those ideas were developed and justified;
- the basic vocabulary, especially technical terms, used in discussion of those ideas;
- some of the key debates that have influenced Christian thinking during the last two thousand years;
- some of the leading thinkers who have shaped Christian theology down the centuries.

It also encourages you to *interact* with these ideas, by helping you to engage with some texts setting out some approaches to these questions. By the time you finish this book, you will be able to go on to deal with more advanced works in the field, including the two standard theological primers written by the present author.

Theology: The Basics builds on the success of two earlier textbooks from the present author and publisher: *Christian Theology: An Introduction* and *The Christian Theology Reader*. The former, now in its third edition, provides a thorough university-level introduction to Christian theology, including comprehensive coverage of the history of theology, the basics of theological method, and detailed engagement with ten major areas of theology. The latter, now in its second edition, provides more than three hundred primary texts of relevance to the study of theology, along with individual introductions, commentary and study questions. Although the present book is intended to be a brief introduction to the themes of Christian theology, it can also be used to lay the groundwork for a more detailed engagement with these two textbooks. The work tries to avoid any form of denominational bias, and aims to treat all positions examined respectfully and fairly.

The approach adopted in this book has been tested on student audiences in Oxford over several years, and I am grateful to those who have helped me evaluate it.

Alister McGrath
Oxford

Getting Started

Theology is "talk about God"; Christian theology is "talk about God" from a Christian perspective. It begins by recognizing that Christians have quite distinct ideas about who God is and what God is like. We find these expressed in the Bible, which all Christians regard as being of immense importance to matters of faith. Christian theology can be seen both as the *process* of reflecting on the Bible and weaving together its ideas and themes, and as the *result* of this process of reflection in certain ideas – ideas that are often referred to as "doctrines" (from the Latin word *doctrina*, meaning "teaching").

There are also other documents which Christians regard with great respect, such as the Apostles' Creed and the Nicene Creed. The word "creed" comes from the Latin word *credo*, meaning "I believe." A creed is basically a brief statement of the main points of the Christian faith. These ancient creeds set out some of the basics of the faith, and are often used widely for teaching purposes. Many theologians would argue that Christian theology is the exploration of the basic ideas of these creeds, investigating their basis in the Bible, and their impact on Christian thinking and living.

So how do we go about studying theology? One way of studying theology is to read some theologians, and see what kind of approach they adopt. How do they develop their ideas? How do they assess arguments? How do they use the Bible and other theologians in their approach? Two theologians from the classic era of Christian theology might be mentioned here:

- Thomas Aquinas (ca. 1225–74), a great theologian of the Middle Ages, whose *Summa Theologiae* (Latin for "Totality of Theology") is one of the most admired works of systematic theology.
- John Calvin (1509–64), whose *Institutes of the Christian Religion* is a landmark in Protestant theology.

In the twentieth century, two theologians are often singled out as being of especial interest:

- The Protestant writer Karl Barth (1886–1968), whose *Church Dogmatics* are often regarded as the most important theological publication of this period.
- The Catholic theologian Karl Rahner (1904–84), whose *Theological Investigations* reestablished the short theological essay as a major way of conducting theological debate and exploration.

This approach has many merits. It does, however, make considerable demands on students. For a start, these writings are often rather long. In addition, you need to know a lot of background material before you can really make sense of them.

For this reason, some writers suggest that a *historical* approach is better. This means looking at the history of Christian theology, and seeing how it developed down the ages. Instead of focusing on a single individual, this approach allows students to see how Christian thinking has evolved. Again, it is a good way of doing theology. Yet it makes huge demands on students. Two thousand years of history takes a long time to master!

That history is often broken down into sections, to make it more manageable. While every theologian will have views on how best to divide two thousand years of Christian history, many use a framework which looks something like this.

The first hundred years is often referred to as the *apostolic* period. This is the period during which the works now included in the New Testament were written. During this time, Christianity was spreading throughout the Mediterranean region and beyond. The missionary journeys of St. Paul, described in the Acts of the Apostles, are an excellent example of this activity.

This is followed by the *patristic* period, which is usually held to begin about the year 100, and end with the Council of Chalcedon in 451. This council marked a landmark in Christian thinking, especially over the identity of Jesus Christ, and is seen by many writers as bringing this important period of theological development to a close. The unusual word "patristic" derives from the Greek word *pater* ("father"), and designates a group of writers who are often collectively known as the "fathers of the church." (Sadly, there were very few women among them.) The patristic period witnessed important theological explorations of the doctrine of the church, the identity of Jesus Christ, the doctrine of the Trinity, and the relation of grace and free will.

This is followed by the *medieval* period, which is widely regarded as extending from the Council of Chalcedon until about the year 1500. This long period was immensely productive theologically, and produced some theological giants. We have already noted Thomas Aquinas' great thirteenth-century work, the *Summa Theologiae*. Many other examples could be set alongside this, such as the writings of Duns Scotus and William of Ockham. Among the many issues to be explored in detail during this period were the relation between faith and reason, and the theology of the sacraments. Alongside this, of course, there was continuing exploration of issues debated during the patristic period, including the identity of Christ and the relation of grace and free will.

The sixteenth century marked a period of radical change in the Western church. This period of *reformation* witnessed the birth of the Protestant reformation, associated with writers such as Martin Luther and John Calvin, which opened up a period of new theological debate. Certain theological topics became particularly hot around this time, especially the place of the Bible in theological debate, the doctrine of the church, and the question of what it is necessary to do in order to be saved. The Catholic church also went through a period of reformation around this time, with the Council of Trent setting out the definitive Catholic position on issues of importance. Many scholars also include the seventeenth century in this period, arguing that this represents the Protestant and Catholic consolidation of the developments that began in the previous century. It was during this century that Christians emigrated to North America, and began to establish that region as a major player in theological debates.

Finally, the *modern* period designates the period since then. This was a period of considerable instability in Western Europe, especially following the French Revolution of 1789, and later through the rise of Marxism in Eastern Europe in the twentieth century. Despite these anxieties, it was a period of remarkable theological creativity throughout Western Europe and North America. In addition, a growing Christian presence in Africa and Asia during the twentieth century led to an increasing interest in developing "local theologies" in these new regions. These local theologies would be grounded in the Christian tradition, but sensitive to their local situations.

To survey these developments, which have been sketched with extreme brevity in these paragraphs, would be an impossible task. The end result would be very superficial and unsatisfactory. For this reason, a historical approach has not been adopted in this work. While studying the history of theology is a fascinating thing to do, it needs to be done in much greater depth than this brief work allows. Happily, there is another way of introducing theology, which avoids this problem.

The approach adopted in this work is *topical*. We are going to look at a number of areas of Christian thought, and explore what

Christian theologians have said about them, and how they developed those ideas. This allows us to begin to wrestle with some of the great questions of Christian theology in a manageable way. It allows you to develop tools to think about theological issues, rather than just learning what certain great theologians have thought about them.

Any serious engagement with theology is going to involve topics, individual theologians, and the history of theology. It is impossible to do theology properly without being aware of what theologians have thought about things in the past, and how this might be relevant today. A short book like this cannot hope to do justice to the complexities of individual thinkers or history. Yet the topical approach will allow us to look at the history of a debate, where this is relevant to the topic being discussed, and also at individual theologians, when they have a particular contribution to make to the discussion. This volume provides two useful additional resources to help with this process of interaction: a brief glossary of theological terms, and the biographical details of the major theologians mentioned in the text.

Throughout its long history, Christian theology has made an appeal to three fundamental resources: the Bible, tradition, and reason. The topical approach allows us to explore the place of each of these resources in theological debate. In view of their importance, we shall examine each of them in a little detail, before moving on to our first topic.

Introducing the Bible

The word "Bible" comes from the Greek word *biblia* ("books"). It refers to a collection of books which Christians regard as having authority in matters of thought and life. The Bible is divided into two major sections, known as the *Old Testament* and the *New Testament*. "Old Testament" is the Christian way of referring to a series of books regarded as authoritative by Judaism, and sometimes known as the Hebrew Bible. The word "testament" needs explanation. In this context, the word really means "covenant" or "dispensation." The basic Christian ideas which underlie this choice of words are:

1 The same God who called the people of Israel also called the Christian church. Both are "chosen peoples," to use the biblical language.
2 A new phase in God's dealings with humanity came about in Jesus Christ. This is usually referred to as a "new covenant" or "new dispensation."

This has important implications for the Christian reading of the Old Testament. For Christians, the Old Testament anticipates the coming of Christ. This idea is regularly developed in the New Testament. If you would like to explore this briefly, read the first two chapters of the Gospel according to Matthew, the first book of the New Testament, and try answering these two questions:

1 How many times does a phrase like "this took place to fulfill the prophecy of . . . " occur in these two chapters?
2 Why do you think that Matthew regards it as so important that Jesus Christ fulfills Old Testament prophecy?

There is widespread agreement within Christianity that the Bible has unique importance in theological debate and personal devotion. All the Protestant confessions of faith stress the centrality of the Bible. More recently, the Second Vatican Council (1962–5) reaffirmed its importance for Catholic theology and preaching. The authority of the Bible is seen as linked with the idea of "inspiration" – in other words, that in some way, the words of the Bible convey the words of God. This is stated clearly by most Protestant confessions of faith, such as the "Gallic Confession of Faith" (1559), which includes the following declaration:

> We believe that the Word contained in these books has proceeded from God, and receives its authority from him alone, and not from human beings.

The *Catechism of the Catholic Church* (1992) sets out a similar position:

> God is the author of Sacred Scripture. The divine revealed realities, which are contained and presented in the text of Sacred Scripture, have been written down under the inspiration of the Holy Spirit. For Holy Mother Church, relying on the faith of the apostolic age, accepts as sacred and canonical the books of the Old and the New Testaments, whole and entire, with all their parts, on the grounds that, written under the inspiration of the Holy Spirit, they have God as their author and have been handed on as such to the Church herself. God inspired the human authors of the sacred books.

There are some disagreements within Christianity over exactly what is included in the Bible. The most important of these concerns a group of works usually referred to as the "Apocrypha" or as "Deuterocanonical works." This includes books such as the Wisdom of Solomon and the Book of Judith. The key point is that these books, though dating from the period of the Old Testament, were not originally written in the Hebrew language.

Protestants tend to regard these books as informative, but not of doctrinal importance. Catholics, on the other hand, regard them as part of the text of the Bible. This difference is reflected in the way in which Protestant and Catholic Bibles are laid out. Protestant Bibles – such as the famous King James Bible of 1611 or the New International Version – include these texts as a third section of the Bible, known as the "Apocrypha" (from the Greek word for "hidden"). Catholic Bibles – such as the Jerusalem Bible – include them within the Old Testament section of the Bible.

Tradition

A series of controversies in the early church brought home the importance of the concept of tradition. The word "tradition" comes from the Latin term *traditio*, which means "handing over," "handing down," or "handing on." It is a thoroughly biblical idea; we find St. Paul reminding his readers that he was handing on to them core teachings of the Christian faith which he had himself received from other people (1 Corinthians 15:1–4). The term can refer to both the action of passing teachings on to others – something which Paul insists must be done within the church – and to the body of teachings passed on in this manner. Tradition can thus be understood as a *process* as well as a *body of teaching*. The Pastoral Epistles (three New Testament letters that are particularly concerned with questions of church structure, and the passing on of Christian teaching: 1 Timothy, 2 Timothy, and Titus), in particular, stress the importance of "guarding the good deposit which was entrusted to you" (2 Timothy 1:14). The New Testament also uses the notion of tradition in a negative sense, meaning something like "human ideas and practices which are not divinely authorized." Thus, Jesus Christ was openly critical of certain human traditions within Judaism (e.g., see Matthew 15:1–6; Mark 7:13).

The importance of the idea of tradition first became obvious in a controversy which broke out during the second century. The Gnostic controversy centered on a number of questions, including how salvation was to be achieved. Christian writers found themselves having to deal with some highly unusual and creative interpretations of the Bible. How were they to deal with these? If the Bible was to be regarded as authoritative, was every interpretation of the Bible to be regarded as of equal value?

Irenaeus of Lyons, one of the church's greatest theologians, did not think so. The question of how the Bible was to be interpreted was of the greatest importance. Heretics, he argued, interpreted the Bible according to their own taste. Orthodox believers, in contrast, interpreted the Bible in ways that their apostolic authors would have approved. What had been handed down from the apostles through the church was not merely the biblical texts themselves, but a certain way of reading and understanding those texts:

Everyone who wishes to perceive the truth should consider the apostolic tradition, which has been made known in every church in the entire world. We are able to number those who are bishops appointed by the apostles, and their successors in the churches to the present day, who taught and knew nothing of such things as these people imagine.

Irenaeus' point is that a continuous stream of Christian teaching, life and interpretation can be traced from the time of the apostles to his own period. The church is able to point to those who have maintained the teaching of the church, and to certain public standard creeds which set out the main lines of Christian belief. Tradition is thus the guarantor of faithfulness to the original apostolic teaching, a safeguard against the innovations and misrepresentations of biblical texts on the part of the Gnostics.

This development is of major importance, as it underlies the emergence of "creeds" – public, authoritative statements of the basic points of the Christian faith, which are based upon the Bible, but avoid maverick interpretations of biblical material. This point was further developed in the early fifth century by Vincent of Lérins, who was concerned that certain doctrinal innovations were being introduced without good reason. There was a need to have public standards by which such doctrines could be judged. So what standard was available, by which the church could be safeguarded from such errors? For Vincent, the answer was clear: tradition. Tradition was "a rule for the interpretation of the prophets and the apostles in such a way that is directed by the rule of the universal church."

Creeds

Having noted the importance of creeds, we may explore how they came about in their present forms. Their emergence was stimulated by two factors of great importance:

1   The need for public statements of faith which could be used
    in teaching and defense of the Christian faith against misrep-
    resentations.
2   The need for personal "confessions of faith" at the time of
    baptism.

We have already touched on the first point; the second needs
further exploration. It is known that the early church attached
enormous importance to the baptism of new members. In the
third and fourth centuries, a definite pattern of instruction and
baptism developed: new members of the church were instructed
in the basics of the Christian faith during the period of Lent, and
baptized on Easter Day. These new members of the church were
asked to confirm their faith by assenting to key statements of
Christian belief.

According to Hippolytus' *Apostolic Tradition*, which dates from
the early years of the third century, we know that three questions
were put to each baptismal candidate: "Do you believe in God, the
Father Almighty? Do you believe in Jesus Christ, our Savior? Do
you believe in the Holy Spirit, the holy church, and the forgiveness
of sins?" As time went on, these questions were gradually changed
into a statement of faith, which each candidate was asked to affirm.

The most important creed to emerge from these "baptismal
creeds" is the Apostles' Creed, which is widely used in Christian
worship today. Traditionally, this creed is set out as twelve statements, each of which is attributed to one of the twelve apostles.
Although it is now widely agreed that this creed was not actually
written by the apostles themselves, it is nevertheless "apostolic"
in the sense that it contains the main ideas of the Christian faith
that the church received from those apostles. The present form of
the creed can be traced to the eighth century. In its present form,
it reads as follows:

> I believe in God, the Father almighty, the creator of heaven and
> earth.
>   I believe in Jesus Christ, God's only Son, our Lord, who was
> conceived by the Holy Spirit, born of the Virgin Mary, suffered

under Pontius Pilate, was crucified, died, and was buried. He descended to the dead. On the third day he rose again; he ascended into heaven, he is seated at the right hand of the Father, and he will come again to judge the living and the dead.

I believe in the Holy Spirit, the holy catholic church, the communion of saints, the forgiveness of sins, the resurrection of the body, and the life everlasting. Amen.

Note that the creed still falls into three parts, corresponding to the three questions that Hippolytus reports as being asked of baptismal candidates back in the third century. Although each of the questions has been expanded, the same basic structure can still be identified.

The Apostles' Creed offers a very convenient summary of some of the main topics of the Christian faith, and we shall regularly use it as a basis for discussion throughout this book.

Reason

Finally, we need to note the importance of reason in Christian theology. Traditionally, Christian theology has seen reason as operating in a subservient role to revelation. Thomas Aquinas argued that supernatural truths needed to be revealed to us. Human reason, on its own, could not hope to gain access to divine mysteries. It could, however, reflect on them, once they had been revealed. This has been the position adopted by most Christian theologians. Reason allows us to reflect on revelation.

During the great "Age of Reason" in Western culture – which most historians suggest is to be dated to the two hundred years between 1750 and 1950 – this judgment was challenged. Reason, it was argued, was capable of deducing anything that needed to be known about God. There was no need to propose divine revelation. Instead, we could rely totally upon reason. This position is generally known as "rationalism" and is still encountered today in some quarters.

There is, of course, continued interest today in the role of reason in theology. The most obvious sign of this is the ongoing debate over "arguments for the existence of God." Although it is very much open to question whether these arguments prove very much, let alone the existence of the Christian god, the fact that there is so much interest in them demonstrates that there is a continuing role for reason in theological debate. We shall consider some of these arguments briefly at a later point in this book.

We now turn to consider one of the most interesting aspects of the relation of faith and reason: the use of "helpmates" or "dialogue partners" in theology, often referred to using the Latin term *ancilla theologiae*, a phrase which literally means "a handmaid of theology."

The "Handmaid": Dialogue Between Theology and Culture

There is a long tradition within Christian theology of drawing on intellectual resources outside the Christian tradition as a means of developing a theological vision. This approach, usually referred to using the Latin phrase *ancilla theologiae*, is grounded in the basic idea that philosophical systems can be a very helpful way of stimulating theological development, and enabling a dialogue to be opened up between Christian thinkers and their surrounding culture. The two most important historical examples of this approach to theology are the dialogues with Platonism and Aristotelianism.

The dialogue with Platonism was of immense importance during the first five centuries of the Christian church, especially in the Greek-speaking world of the Eastern Mediterranean. As Christianity expanded in that region, it encountered rival worldviews, of which Platonism was the most important. Such worldviews could be seen positively or negatively: they were both an opportunity for dialogue and intellectual development, and also a threat to the existence of Christianity. The task faced by writers such as Justin Martyr or Clement of Alexandria was how to make use of the obvious intellectual merits of Platonism in constructing a Christian worldview, without compromising the integrity of Christianity itself. After all, despite their occasional similarities, Christianity is *not* Platonism.

A new debate opened up in the thirteenth century, during the golden age of scholastic theology. The rediscovery of Aristotle by medieval writers seemed to offer new resources to help in every aspect of intellectual life, including physics, philosophy and ethics. It was inevitable that theologians should also want to see what use they could make of Aristotelian ideas and methods in constructing a systematic theology – such as Thomas Aquinas' massive *Summa Theologiae*, widely regarded as one of the greatest works of theology ever written.

In both these cases, using another intellectual discipline as the *ancilla theologiae* offers opportunities and risks in about equal measure. It is clearly important to appreciate what these opportunities and risks are. The two major *opportunities* offered to theology can be summarized as follows:

1 It allows for a much more rigorous exploration of ideas than would otherwise be possible. Problems that Christian theology encounters in trying to develop its ideas often have their parallels in other disciplines. Thomas Aquinas, for example, found Aristotle's notion of an "unmoved mover" helpful in setting out some reasons for defending the existence of God.
2 It allows Christian theology to engage in a dialogue with another worldview – a major element of the church's witness to its secular context. In the second century, Justin Martyr clearly believed that many Platonists would be so impressed by the parallels between Platonism and Christianity that they might consider conversion. Similarly, in his "Areopagus address" (Acts 17:22–31), Paul draws on some themes from Stoic philosophy in attempting to communicate the Christian message to Athenian culture.

Alongside these positive aspects, an obvious risk must also be noted: ideas which are not distinctively Christian come to play a significant (perhaps even decisive) role in Christian theology. For example, Aristotelian ideas about the proper manner of logical reasoning, or Cartesian ideas about the proper starting point for any intellectual discipline, might find their way into Christian theology. On some occasions, this might turn out to be a neutral development; on others, it may eventually be recognized to have negative implications, undermining the integrity of Christian theology, and ultimately causing it to be distorted. Martin Luther, the great German reformer, argued that medieval theology had allowed a number of such distortions to arise through an excessive, and partially uncritical, use of Aristotelian ideas in the Middle Ages.

Despite these concerns, the approach continues to be widely used. Many German theologians of the nineteenth century found the work of the philosophers G. W. F. Hegel and Immanuel Kant to be helpful dialogue partners. In the twentieth century, Rudolf Bultmann and Paul Tillich both found a dialogue with existentialism to be theologically productive. More recently, I myself have argued that the working methods and assumptions of the natural sciences can be theologically significant (see my three-volume work *A Scientific Theology*).

Moving On

This section has sketched something of the background to Christian theology. Yet it has left huge areas completely untouched. The best way of filling in these many gaps is to begin to explore some specific theological topics, and use these as ways of reflecting on some of the issues, ideas, personalities, and debates of Christian theology. To do this, we shall use a framework. Rather than just explore issues at random, we will allow the structure of the Apostles' Creed to set boundaries to our reflections.

In making this decision, I have been influenced by two particular considerations. Many users of this book will be taking part in church or college study groups, where the Apostles' Creed is an obvious reference point for discussion. Many colleges teach courses in basic Christian doctrine using the Apostles' Creed to frame the lectures, which will allow this book to be helpful background reading. However, the basic approach of the book does not tie it down in any particular way. The topics identified for further exploration are of wide theological interest, irrespective of the context in which you are studying them.

So where shall we begin? The obvious place is to consider what it means to say that we "believe" in God. The Apostles' Creed opens with the words "I believe." So what does this mean? And what issues does it raise? We may turn immediately to explore these questions.

CHAPTER 1

Faith ✓

"I believe in God." This terse opening phrase of the Apostles' Creed leads us directly into our first theological topic. What does it mean to talk about "believing in God"? What are we to understand by words such as "belief" and "faith"?

The biblical sense of the word "faith" has a number of aspects. One biblical theme is of particular importance: the idea of trusting in God, related in the famous Old Testament account of the calling of Abraham (Genesis 15:1–6). This tells how God promised to give Abraham countless descendants, as numerous as the stars of the night sky. Abraham believed God – that is, trusted the promise that was made to him. Similarly, the crowds around Jesus are often described as having "faith" – meaning that they believed that he had some special status, identity, or authority, and would be able to heal them from their illnesses, or deal with their concerns (e.g., Luke 5:20; 17:19). Here again the basic idea is trust, in this case mingled with discernment that there is something about Jesus which merits such an attitude of trust.

In everyday language, words like "faith" and "belief" have come to mean something like "a weak form of knowledge."

I know that the chemical formula for water is H_2O, or that the earth rotates around the sun. When I say "I know" that the capital of the United States of America is Washington, DC, I mean that this statement can be verified. But when I say "I believe in God," this is widely understood to mean something like "I think that there is a God, but I cannot demonstrate this with any degree of certainty."

This everyday use of the terms "faith" and "belief" is misleading, however, as it does not do justice to the complexity of the theological notion of "faith." In the eighteenth and nineteenth centuries, Western philosophy widely believed that anything worth believing could be *proved* – whether by logical reasoning, or by scientific experimentation. As the great nineteenth-century mathematician W. K. Clifford (1845–79), argued: "It is wrong always, everywhere, and for anyone, to believe anything upon insufficient evidence." This "positivism" had a deep impact on Western culture, and its influence still lingers. The idea of "faith in God" was ridiculed by some rationalist writers, who argued that unless God's existence could be proved, there was no reason to pay the slightest attention to this alleged divinity.

Yet with the passing of time, the credibility of this position has been severely weakened. It has become increasingly clear that many of the fundamental beliefs of Western culture lie beyond proof. The philosopher of science Michael Polanyi pointed out that certain unprovable beliefs lay behind the working methods of the natural sciences. As Alfred Lord Tennyson (1809–92) pointed out in his poem *The Ancient Sage*, nothing that was actually worth believing could be proved in the way that people like Clifford demanded:

> For nothing worthy proving can be proven,
> Nor yet disproven: wherefore thou be wise,
> Cleave ever to the sunnier side of doubt.

Since then, philosophers have become much more realistic. Some things can indeed be proved; but some, by their very nature, lie beyond proof. God is one of these.

The basic Christian attitude to proofs for the existence of God can be set out as follows:

1 The existence of God is something that reason cannot prove conclusively. Yet the fact that the existence of God lies *beyond* reason does not for one moment mean that the existence of God is *contrary* to reason.
2 Certain excellent reasons may be put forward for suggesting that God exists; these do not, however, count as "proofs" in the sense of "rigorous logical demonstrations" or "conclusive scientific experiments."
3 Faith is about trust in God, rather than just agreeing that God exists.

We have already begun to move towards talking about "proofs" for God's existence. In what follows, we shall explore this aspect of Christian theology in a little more detail, focusing on the ideas of Thomas Aquinas, one of Christianity's most interesting theologians.

Proofs of God's Existence?

Thomas Aquinas (ca. 1225–74) is probably the most famous and influential theologian of the Middle Ages. Born in Italy, he achieved his fame through his teaching and writing at the University of Paris and other Northern universities. His fame rests chiefly on his *Summa Theologiae*, composed towards the end of his life and not totally finished at the time of his death. However, he also wrote many other significant works, particularly the *Summa contra Gentiles*, which represents a major statement of the rationality of the Christian faith, and especially the existence of God. Aquinas believed it was entirely proper to identify pointers towards the existence of God, drawn from general human experience of the world. His "Five Ways" represent five lines of argument in support of the existence of God, each of which draws on some aspect of the world which "points" to the existence of its creator.

So what kind of pointers does Aquinas identify? The basic line of thought guiding Aquinas is that the world mirrors God as its creator – an idea which is given more formal expression in his doctrine of the "analogy of being." Just as an artist might sign a painting to identify it as his handiwork, so God has written a divine "signature" upon creation. What we observe in the world –for example, its signs of ordering – can be explained if God was its creator. If God both brought the world into existence, and stamped the divine image and likeness upon it, then something of God's nature can be known from creation.

So where might we look in creation to find evidence for the existence of God? Aquinas argues that the ordering of the world is the most convincing evidence of God's existence and wisdom. This basic assumption underlies each of the Five Ways, although it is of particular importance in the case of the argument often referred to as the "argument from design" or the "teleological argument." We shall consider the first and last of these two "ways" to illustrate the issues.

The first way begins from the observation that things in the world are in motion or change. The world is not static, but is dynamic. Examples of this are easy to list. Rain falls from the sky. Stones roll down valleys. The earth revolves around the sun (a fact, incidentally, unknown to Aquinas). This, the first of Aquinas' arguments, is normally referred to as the "argument from motion"; however, it is clear that the "movement" in question is actually understood in more general terms, so that the term "change" is more appropriate as a translation.

So how did nature come to be in motion? Why is it changing? Why isn't it static? Aquinas argues that everything which moves is moved by something else. For every motion, there is a cause. Things don't just move; they are moved by something else. Now, each cause of motion must itself have a cause. And that cause must have a cause as well. And so Aquinas argues that there is a whole series of causes of motion lying behind the world as we know it. Unless there is an infinite number of these causes, Aquinas argues, there must be a single cause right at the origin of the series. From this original cause of motion, all other motion is ultimately derived. This is the origin of the great chain of causality which we see reflected in the way the world behaves. From the fact that things are in motion, Aquinas thus argues for the existence of a single original cause of all this motion. This, Aquinas insists, is none other than God.

In more recent times, this argument has been restated in terms of God as the one who brought the universe into existence. For this reason, it is often referred to as the "cosmological" argument (from the Greek word *kosmos*, meaning "universe"). The most commonly encountered statement of the argument runs along the following lines:

1   Everything within the universe depends on something else for its existence.
2   What is true of its individual parts is also true of the universe itself.
3   The universe thus depends on something else for its existence for as long as it has existed or will exist.
4   The universe thus depends on God for its existence.

The argument basically assumes that the existence of the universe is something that requires explanation. It will be clear that this type of argument relates directly to modern cosmological research, particularly the "big bang" theory of the origins of the cosmos.

The fifth and final way is known as the "teleological argument," which derives its name from the Greek word *telos*, meaning "purpose" or "goal." Aquinas notes that the world shows obvious traces of intelligent design. Natural processes and objects seem to be adapted with certain definite objectives in mind. They seem to have a purpose. They seem to have been designed. But things don't design themselves: they are caused and designed by someone or something else. Arguing from this observation, Aquinas concludes that the source of this natural ordering must be conceded to be God.

This argument was developed by William Paley (1743–1805). According to Paley, the world was like a watch. It showed evidence of intelligent design, and having been created for a purpose. If there was a watch, there must also be a watchmaker. Paley was particularly impressed by the construction of the human eye, which he argued was so complex and highly developed that it could only be the result of intelligent design and construction.

Paley's argument was highly influential in nineteenth-century England. However, its plausibility was eroded by Charles Darwin's (1809–82) theory of evolution, which offered an alternative explanation of how such complex structures arose. In his *Origin of Species* (1859), Darwin insisted that these could be explained on a purely natural basis, without need for an intelligent divine designer. Nevertheless, the "argument from design" remains an intriguing idea, which continues to fascinate people.

It will be obvious that Aquinas' arguments are similar in terms of their structure. Each depends on tracing a causal sequence back to its single origin, and identifying this with God. These are thus not "proofs" in the strict sense of the word, as they actually presuppose God's existence! Aquinas' approach is actually rather different. His argument is that, if we presuppose that God made the world, we end up with a way of making sense of the world that makes a lot of sense of things. In other words, Aquinas is arguing that, seen from the Christian perspective, the existence of God resonates well with what can be observed of the world. It is thus a confirmation, but not a proof, of God's existence.

However, other theologians have viewed such "proofs" with skepticism. The great French mathematician and philosopher Blaise Pascal (1623–62) had two major concerns about the kind of approach adopted by Aquinas. First, he found it difficult to accept that the rather abstract philosophical "god" which resulted from such arguments was anything like the living God of the Old and New Testaments. In his *Pensées*, Pascal put it like this: "The metaphysical proofs for the existence of God are so remote from human reasoning, and so complex, that they have little impact."

Second, Pascal argued that these "proofs" assumed that God was known primarily through reason. For Pascal, the human heart also had its reasons for believing (or not believing!) in God. "We know the truth, not only through our reason, but also through our heart." The appeal of God to the human condition went far beyond any resonance between the world as we know it and the ideas of the Christian faith. It extends to include a deep-seated longing for God, which Pascal held to be of major importance in the long, unended human quest for God and final meaning.

In the end, according to Pascal, you cannot argue someone into the Kingdom of God. The existence of God is not something that can be proved. Equally, it is not something that can be *disproved*. It is easy to overlook the fact that atheism is also a faith. An atheist believes that there is no God. This belief, however, is just as difficult to prove as the Christian belief that there is indeed a God.

Faith is Beyond Reason But Not Contrary to Reason

One of the most important recent discussions of the relation of faith and reason is found in Pope John Paul II's 1998 encyclical letter *Fides et Ratio* ("Faith and Reason"). This letter sets out the classic Christian approach to the relation of faith and reason in a very accessible way. In what follows, we shall explore this import- ant document's arguments.

The letter opens with a declaration that faith and reason can work together. "Faith and reason are like two wings on which the human spirit rises to the contemplation of truth; and God has placed in the human heart a desire to know the truth – in a word, to know himself – so that, by knowing and loving God, men and women may also come to the fullness of truth about themselves." This is a rich and powerful statement, which deserves close atten- tion. The basic idea is that human beings long to know the truth, and are constantly searching for it. "In the far reaches of the human heart there is a seed of desire and nostalgia for God."

So can reason alone lead humanity to this truth? The letter pays a handsome tribute to philosophy, as the legitimate human quest for truth. Philosophy is "one of the noblest of human tasks," which is "driven by the desire to discover the ultimate truth of existence." Yet unaided human reason cannot fully penetrate to the mystery of life. It cannot answer questions such as "why are we here?" For this reason, God graciously chose to make these things known through revelation which would otherwise remain unknown. "The truth made known to us by Revelation is neither the product nor the consummation of an argument devised by human reason."

The letter stresses that faith is not blind trust, opposed to the evidence of the world. Rather, it points out that the world – which Christians see as God's creation – is studded with hints of God's existence and nature. It appeals to St. Paul's sermon preached at the Areopagus in Athens (Acts 17) in arguing that it is entirely reasonable to infer the existence of God from the wonders of nature and a human sense of divinity within us. These do not count as "proofs"; they are, however, confirmation or corroboration of the basic themes of faith. In the eleventh century, Anselm of Canterbury argued that "faith seeks understanding." Having believed, we long to understand the inner dynamics and structures of our faith.

Similar lines of argument are developed by John Polkinghorne, one of Britain's leading theoretical physicists with a strong interest in Christian theology. Throughout his many books, Polkinghorne stresses that Christianity, like the natural sciences, is concerned about making sense of the world on the basis of the evidence that is available. "Faith is not a question of shutting one's eyes, gritting one's teeth, and believing the impossible. It involves a leap, but a leap into the light rather than the dark." Faith is to be understood as "motivated belief, based on evidence." It is rigorously based on reflection on the world – on the various "clues" it offers to its origins and nature.

For example, Polkinghorne argues that science shows us a universe that is deeply intelligible, rationally beautiful, finely tuned for fruitfulness, intrinsically rational, partly veiled in character, open in its process and information-generating in its nature. These remarkable properties, he argues, are not just happy accidents. They are something that needs to be explained. For Polkinghorne, the best explanation of these observations is that the world is the orderly creation of God. The approach is evidence-based, asking how what we observe may best be explained. It is not conclusive; it is, however, highly suggestive.

Polkinghorne also stresses the importance of the figure of Jesus of Nazareth for Christian faith. Jesus is part of the evidence that has to be assessed:

> The center of my faith lies in my encounter with the figure of Jesus Christ, as I meet him in the gospels, in the witness of the church and in the sacraments. Here is the heart of my Christian faith and hope. Yet, at a subsidiary but supportive level, there are also hints of God's presence which arise from our scientific knowledge. The actual way we answer the question "How?" turns out to point us on to pressing also the question "Why?," so that science by itself is found not to be sufficiently intellectually satisfying.

Although some atheist writers persist in portraying Christian faith as a blind leap in the dark, it is clear that this is not the case. Faith, as Thomas Aquinas points out, has its reasons.

Up to this point, we have considered faith primarily in terms of intellectual assent. For Thomas Aquinas, faith could be defined as "assent to divine revelation." Yet there is more to the idea than this. During the sixteenth century, particular emphasis came to be placed on the relational aspects of faith. To "believe in God" is about more than accepting that God exists; it is about *trusting* that God. In what follows, we shall consider this important aspect of faith.

Faith and God's Promises

Martin Luther (1483–1546) is one of a number of writers who stressed that faith, as the Christian church understands the term, is far more than intellectual assent. Certainly, faith believes that certain things are true. There is unquestionably an element of understanding to faith. But there is more to it than that. For

Luther, faith is fundamentally trust. He often uses the Latin word *fiducia*, which could be translated as "confidence," to denote the aspect of faith he wants to emphasize. Faith is about trusting a God who makes promises, and whose promises may be relied upon. In his major 1520 essay *The Babylonian Captivity of the Church*, Luther stressed this aspect of faith:

> Where there is the Word of the God who makes promises, there must necessarily be the faith of the person who accepts those promises. It is clear that the beginning of our salvation is a faith which clings to the Word of a promising God who, without any effort on our part, in free and unmerited mercy goes before us and offers us a word of promise.

Three points relating to Luther's idea of faith may be singled out for discussion:

1 Faith has a personal, rather than a purely historical, reference.
2 Faith concerns trust in the promises of God.
3 Faith unites the believer to Christ.

We shall consider each of these points individually.

First, faith is not simply historical knowledge. Luther argues that a faith which is content to believe in the historical reliability of the gospels is not a faith which changes our relationship with God. Sinners are perfectly capable of trusting in the historical details of the gospels; but these facts of themselves are not adequate for true Christian faith. Saving faith concerns believing and trusting that Christ was born for us personally, and has accomplished for us the work of salvation. As Luther puts this point:

> I have often spoken about two different kinds of faith. The first of them is like this: you believe that it is true that Christ is the person who is described and proclaimed in the gospels, but you do not believe that he is such a person for you. You doubt if you can receive that from him, and you think: "Yes, I'm sure he is that person for someone else (like Peter and Paul, and for religious and

holy people). But is he that person for me? Can I confidently expect to receive everything from him that the saints expect?" You see, this faith is nothing. It receives nothing of Christ, and tastes nothing of him either. It cannot feel joy, nor love of him or for him. This is a faith related to Christ, but not a faith in Christ . . . The only faith which deserves to be called Christian is this: you believe unreservedly that it is not only for Peter and the saints that Christ is such a person, but also for you yourself – in fact, for you more than anyone else.

The second point concerns faith as trust (Latin: *fiducia*). This notion of faith is prominent in the sixteenth-century conception of faith, and occurs frequently in the writings of both Luther and Calvin. Luther uses a nautical analogy to bring out the importance of trust and commitment in the life of faith: "Everything depends upon faith. The person who does not have faith is like someone who has to cross the sea, but is so frightened that he does not trust the ship. And so he stays where he is, and is never saved, because he will not get on board and cross over." Faith is not merely believing that something is true; it is being prepared to act upon that belief, and rely upon it. To use Luther's analogy: faith is not simply about believing that a ship exists; it is about stepping into it, and entrusting ourselves to it.

But what are we being asked to trust? Are we being asked simply to have faith in faith? The question could perhaps be phrased more accurately: who are we being asked to trust? For Luther, the answer was unequivocal: faith is about being prepared to put one's trust in the promises of God, and the integrity and faithfulness of the God who made those promises. Believers "must be certain that the one who has promised forgiveness to whoever confesses their sins will most faithfully fulfill this promise." For Luther, faith is only as strong as the one in whom we believe and trust. The efficacy of faith does not rest upon the intensity with which we believe, but in the reliability of the one in whom we believe. It is not the greatness of our faith, but the greatness of God, which counts. As Luther puts it:

> Even if my faith is weak, I still have exactly the same treasure and
> the same Christ as others. There is no difference . . . It is like two
> people, each of whom owns a hundred gold coins. One may carry
> them around in a paper sack, the other in an iron chest. But
> despite these differences, they both own the same treasure. Thus
> the Christ who you and I own is one and the same, irrespective of
> the strength or weakness of your faith or mine.

The content of faith matters far more than its intensity. It is
pointless to trust passionately in someone who is not worthy of
trust; even a modicum of faith in someone who is totally reliable
is vastly to be preferred. Trust is not, however, an occasional
attitude. For Luther, it is an undeviating trusting outlook upon
life, a constant stance of conviction of the trustworthiness of the
promises of God. As Karl Barth put this in the twentieth century:
"In God alone is there faithfulness, and faith is the trust that we
may hold to Him, to His promise and to His guidance. To hold
to God is to rely on the fact that God is there for me, and to live
in this certainty."

In the third place, faith unites the believer with Christ. Luther
states this principle clearly in his 1520 writing, *The Liberty of a
Christian*:

> Faith unites the soul with Christ as a bride is united with her
> bridegroom. As Paul teaches us, Christ and the soul become one
> flesh by this mystery (Ephesians 5:31–2). And if they are one flesh,
> and if the marriage is for real – indeed, it is the most perfect of all
> marriages, and human marriages are poor examples of this one true
> marriage – then it follows that everything that they have is held in
> common, whether good or evil. So the believer can boast of and
> glory of whatever Christ possesses, as though it were his or her own;
> and whatever the believer has, Christ claims as his own. Let us see
> how this works out, and see how it benefits us. Christ is full of grace,
> life and salvation. The human soul is full of sin, death and damna-
> tion. Now let faith come between them. Sin, death and damnation
> will be Christ's. And grace, life and salvation will be the believer's.

Faith, then, is not assent to an abstract set of doctrines – which
is perhaps a weakness of Aquinas' approach. Rather, it is a

"wedding ring" (Luther), pointing to mutual commitment and union between Christ and the believer. It is the response of the whole person of the believer to God, which leads in turn to the real and personal presence of Christ in the believer. "To know Christ is to know his benefits," wrote Philip Melanchthon, Luther's colleague at Wittenberg. Faith makes both Christ and his benefits – such as forgiveness, justification, and hope – available to the believer. Calvin makes this point with characteristic clarity: "Having ingrafted us into his body, [Christ] makes us partakers, not only of all his benefits, but also of himself." Christ, Calvin insists, is not "received merely in the understanding and imagination. For the promises offer him, not so that we end up with the mere sight and knowledge of him, but that we enjoy a true communication of him."

Engaging With a Text

In this opening chapter, we have explored some aspects of faith. We have seen how faith can be understood in a number of ways. To believe in God is both about accepting that a God exists, and also that this God can be known and trusted. We have already looked at some ideas in the writings of Thomas Aquinas and Martin Luther to illustrate these points. Now we are going to try to take things further, and interact with a theological text.

Why is this so important? Because at some point, you are going to need to begin reading works of theology for yourself. It is therefore important to begin interacting with these in a manageable way as soon as possible. Some chapters of this book have a section which will help you to engage with a short extract from a leading theologian or theological document. These will be drawn from a variety of Christian traditions, offering you experience of a number of different approaches. You will be guided through this process. To begin with, the texts will be short – but gradually, they will become longer. Initially, you will be given a lot of help – but as you gain in confidence, there will be less need for this assistance. We are going to begin this process of engagement with a short but fascinating extract from a leading Protestant writer on the theme of faith.

The text in question is John Calvin's *Institutes of the Christian Religion*, which was first published in 1536 and went through many editions until the final, definitive edition of 1559. Calvin is a very precise and logical theologian, who is generally very easy to read and understand. In what follows, we are going to interact with the definition of faith which he sets out in this major work. Here is the definition:

> Now we shall have a right definition of faith if we say that it is a steady and certain knowledge of the divine benevolence towards us, which is founded upon the truth of the gracious promise of God in Christ, and is both revealed to our minds and sealed in our hearts by the Holy Spirit.

Take a few moments to read this through, and take in what Calvin is saying. Then use these questions as a way of engaging with his ideas.

1 Note how Calvin's definition of faith is *trinitarian*. We shall explore this aspect of the Christian faith in more detail in chapter 6. For the moment, notice how Calvin ascribes different aspects of faith to each of the three persons of the Trinity – Father, Son, and Spirit. Try to write down what each of these aspects are. If you are studying this book in a discussion group, spend some time talking about this, making sure that you are happy about the threefold structure of this definition.

2 Now note that the first part of this definition declares that faith is a "steady and certain knowledge of the divine benevolence towards us." Notice first how Calvin uses language that expresses confidence in God, and stresses God's reliability. Notice also how faith is defined as

"knowledge" – but a certain very specific kind of knowledge. It is not just "knowledge"; in fact, it is not even "knowledge of God." It is specifically "knowledge of *God's benevolence towards us.*" Calvin's language is very specific and intentional. Faith is grounded and based in God's *goodness.* It is not simply about accepting that God exists, but about encountering God's kindness to us. Do you agree with Calvin at this point?

3   The definition now goes on to declare that faith is "founded upon the truth of the gracious promise of God in Christ." Again, notice how faith is again affirmed to be about knowledge – the use of the word "truth" is very important here. Calvin wants to make it absolutely clear that faith is not a human invention or delusion, but something that is grounded in the bedrock of truth. But notice how Calvin then proceeds to link this with a "gracious promise of God." For Calvin, we are dealing with a God who makes promises to us – promises which can be trusted and relied upon. You might like to compare this idea with Luther's views on the matter, which we considered earlier in this chapter, and notice their similarity at this point. It is important to see how Calvin identifies Christ as the confirmation or means of disclosure of these promises. You might like to look up 2 Corinthians 1:20 and see how Calvin's approach relates to that text.

4   Calvin clearly holds that faith involves both mind and heart. If you are in a discussion group, you might like to explore how he approaches each of these. Note how, once more, Calvin affirms that faith is indeed about knowledge – something that affects the way in which we think, affecting our minds. Yet it is more than this: it is something that transforms us internally. Notice how Calvin's language about the "heart" points to a deeper change within us than just mental acceptance of an idea. Calvin sees God as active throughout the process of coming to faith. Faith is not

human insight; it is personal knowledge of God made possible by the Holy Spirit.

Having explored the meaning of "faith," we may now turn to explore its content, beginning with God.

CHAPTER 2

God ✓

God lies at the heart of Christian theology. But *which* God? And what is this God like? It is clear that the little word "God" needs extensive amplification. Israel's reflections on the identity of its God – which they styled using phrases such as "the Lord God of Israel" – took place against a background of polytheism. Each nation in the region had its own god; many had highly developed pantheons, recognizing many different gods, each with its own distinctive function or sphere of influence. Simply talking about "God" was thus not particularly informative. It begged the question: which of these gods do you mean? Part of the task of Christian theology is to identify the God in which Christians believe.

This process of identification can be seen in both the Old and New Testaments. For the Old Testament prophets, Israel knew and worshipped the God who had brought them out of Egypt, and led them into the promised land. In the New Testament, we find this idea picked up and developed further. Christians believe in the same God as Abraham; this God is, however, finally and fully disclosed in Jesus Christ. Thus, Paul speaks of "the God and Father of our Lord Jesus Christ" (2 Corinthians 1:3).

The basic idea we find throughout the New Testament is that Christians worship and know the same God as Israel. Nevertheless, Christians hold that this God is revealed supremely and finally in Christ. Thus the letter to the Hebrews opens by declaring that the same God who spoke to Israel "in many times and in various ways" through the prophets has now "spoken to us through a Son," who is to be recognized as the "exact representation" of God (Hebrews 1:1–3). This point is of great importance, as it demonstrates how the Christian understanding of God is linked with the person of Christ. To know Christ is to know God. Or, as a second-century Christian writer put it, "we must learn to think of Jesus as of God" (1 Clement 1:1).

So what do Christians believe about this God? The opening words of the Apostles' Creed get us off to a good start: Christians believe in a God who is "the Father Almighty, Creator of heaven and earth." We shall turn to explore the very rich and powerful theme of creation in chapter 3. To begin with, we shall look at the idea of God as "Father Almighty." We can break this down into two segments, each of which really deserves a chapter to itself. However, limits on space mean that we will have to consider them both briefly, beginning with the question of what it means to speak of God as "Father."

Analogies in Theology

One of the most noticeable things about the Christian representation of God is that extensive use is made of imagery. God is depicted as a shepherd, a king, a rock – and a father. Before we begin to explore what it means to talk about God as "father," it will be helpful to look at the general question of the use of analogies in theology.

The Bible uses many analogies to speak about God. To explore some of the issues that arise from using analogies in theology, we may turn to consider one of the most familiar biblical verses in

Psalm 23:1: "The Lord is my shepherd." This image of God as a shepherd is encountered frequently in the Old Testament (e.g., Psalm 80:1; Isaiah 40:11; Ezekiel 34:12), and is taken up in the New Testament to refer to Jesus, who is the "good shepherd" (John 10:11). But what does this analogy tell us about God? How can we develop this image theologically? The easiest way of answering this question is to wrestle with the image, and see what happens. If you are in a discussion group, close this book, and talk about the question which follows. If you're working on your own, write down what comes into your mind in response to the following question.

What ideas come to mind when we talk of a shepherd?

For most people, four ideas come to mind, as follows.

First, there is the idea of the shepherd's loving care for the sheep. The shepherd was committed to his flock of sheep on a full-time basis. Indeed, the shepherd tended to be regarded as a social outcast in Israel, precisely on account of the enormous amount of time he was obliged to spend with his flock, which prevented him from taking part in normal social activities. To speak of God as a shepherd thus conveys the idea of the total commitment of God to Israel and the church. The idea is developed very powerfully in the New Testament, especially in the parable of the lost sheep (Luke 15:3–7) Here the shepherd actively seeks out the lost sheep, in order to bring it home. The final intensification of the image is found in John's gospel, where it is emphasized that the good shepherd – who is immediately identified as Jesus – will willingly go so far as to lay down his life for the safety of his sheep (John 10:11–16).

Second, thinking of God as a shepherd affirms God's guidance. The shepherd knows where food and water are to be found, and guides the sheep to them. To liken God to a shepherd is to emphasize God's constant presence with Israel and the church. It is to affirm God's ability to protect us from the dangers which life offers and to bring people to a place of plenty and safety. God "tends his flock like a shepherd. He gathers the lambs in his arms and carries them close to his heart; he gently leads those that have young" (Isaiah 40:11).

Third, the image of God as shepherd tells us something about ourselves, from a Christian perspective. We are the sheep of God's pasture (Psalms 79:13; 95:7; 100:3). We are like sheep, incapable of looking after ourselves, and continually going astray. We are not self-sufficient: just as the sheep rely upon the shepherd for their existence, so we have to learn to rely upon God. We may like to think that we are capable of looking after ourselves, but a Christian understanding of human nature demands that we recognize our total dependence upon God. Thus, human sinfulness is often compared with running away from God, like a stray sheep. "We all, like sheep, have gone astray; each of us has turned to his own way" (Isaiah 53:6; cf. Psalm 119.176; 1 Peter 2:25).

And fourth, just as the shepherd goes to look for his lost sheep, so God came to find us in our lostness, and bring us home. The parallels with the parable of the prodigal son (Luke 15:11–32) will be obvious. In that gospel chapter, we find three stories of "lost-ness" being turned to "being found" and "rejoicing." The shepherd finds his lost sheep (Luke 15:3–8); the woman finds her lost coin (Luke 15:8–10); the father finds his lost son (Luke 15:11–32). And in all these analogies, we find the same constant emphasis of the Christian faith: that we are lost, and that God has come into the world in Jesus Christ in order to find us, and bring us home.

To speak of "God as a shepherd" is thus to affirm "God is *like* a shepherd." In other words, the image of a shepherd helps us think about the nature of God, and allows us to gain insights into his nature. It does not mean that God is *identical* to a human shepherd. Rather, it means that some aspects of a human shepherd help us think about God more effectively.

But is *every* aspect of the human analogy to be carried over to God? Every analogy breaks down at some point. How far can we press this analogy before it ceases to be reliable? To explore this issue, we could draw up a brief list of things that are true about shepherds:

1   Shepherds look after sheep.
2   Shepherds protect their sheep against danger.
3   Shepherds lead their sheep to food and water.
4   Shepherds are human beings.

It is immediately clear that the first three aspects of the analogy can be carried over to our thinking about God. God cares, protects, and leads. In all these respects, the analogy of the shepherd works well, and illuminates the character of God.

Yet shepherds are ultimately human beings. Is *this* aspect of the analogy to be carried over? It is quite clear we are not meant to think of God as a human being. While God is *not* a human being, it is still true that the behavior of one particular group of human beings is seen as helping us to get a better understanding of the nature of God. So it would seem that this is one aspect of the analogy which we are not meant to press too far.

Now these are very simple points to make, and you might feel that they are out of place in any serious discussion of Christian theology. In fact, this is far from the case. What we have been doing is exploring the important theological issue of how far an analogy of God is to be pressed, and how these analogies can offer powerful visual stimulus to theological reflection. It also raises the question of why we should use images of God in this way. Why not use more conceptual or abstract ways of speaking or thinking about God? The answer within the Christian theological tradition could be summarized as follows.

There is no way in which a created human mind would be capable of beholding God directly. As a result, we need to think of God in a scaled-down manner, appropriate to our ability to cope. Some early Christian writers used to compare understanding God with looking directly into the sun. The human eye is simply not capable of withstanding the full brilliance of the sun. In the same way, the human mind cannot cope with the full glory of God.

The story is told of the pagan emperor who visited the Jewish rabbi Joshua ben Hananiah. The emperor asked to be allowed to see Joshua's god. The rabbi replied that this was impossible, an answer which failed to satisfy the emperor. So the rabbi took the emperor outside, and asked him to stare at the midday summer sun. "Impossible!" replied the emperor. "If you cannot look at the sun, which God created," replied the rabbi, "how much less can you behold the glory of God himself!"

Even though the human eye cannot cope with the full brightness of the sun, however, it is nevertheless possible to look at the sun through a piece of dark glass. This greatly reduces the brilliance of the sun, so that the human eye can cope with it. Otherwise, looking at the sun would be completely beyond its capacities. In much the same way, it is helpful to think of the scriptural models or pictures of God as revealing God in manageable proportions, so that the human mind can cope with him.

John Calvin (1509–64) argued that God knows our limited ability to cope with ideas, and thus reveals himself in ways that we can handle. According to Calvin, God's revelation is adapted or "accommodated" to our capacity for reflection. Calvin insists that God simply cannot be comprehended by the human mind. What is known of God is known by revelation; and that revelation is adapted to our capacity as finite, fallen human creatures. This does not reflect any weakness or inadequacy on God's part. It is simply a reflection of God's generous and kindly nature, by which God takes our weakness into account. Calvin comments that "God accommodates himself to our ability" – meaning that God uses words, ideas, and images that we can relate to.

So having explored the use of analogies in theology, we may now turn to the specific analogy that we encounter in the creed: the analogy of God as a *father*.

God as Father

The image of God as father is deeply embedded within the Christian faith, not least because of the prayer that Christ taught his disciples, now known as the Lord's Prayer. Its opening words will be familiar to many readers: "Our Father . . . " If Jesus Christ referred to God in this way, it is clearly of major importance to Christian faith. But how are we to interpret this image?

Once more, we are dealing with an analogy. So what sort of ideas does the analogy convey? You might like to spend a few moments jotting down some of the ideas that the image conveys, much as we did earlier in the case of the shepherd analogy. The following ideas might come to mind, and we shall explore each of them briefly:

1 Fathers are human beings.
2 Fathers bring their children into existence.
3 Fathers care for their children.
4 Fathers are male.

The first of these characteristics is clearly not meant to be transferred to our thinking about God. As we saw in the case of the shepherd analogy, this is the inevitable consequence of using language drawn from the created order to refer to the creator.

The second is clearly important. God is our originator. Without God, we would not be here. Both the Old and New Testaments stress our complete dependence upon God from beginning to end. There is also no doubt that the analogy of God as father conveys the idea of care. The Old Testament in particular often compares God's relation with his people to a father's relationship with his young son. When the son is very young, he is totally dependent upon his father for everything, and their relationship is very close. But as the son grows older, he gradually comes to exercise his independence and break away from his father, so that the relationship becomes more distant. The prophet Hosea uses this illustration to bring out how Israel has become a virtual stranger to the God who called her into existence:

> When Israel was a child, I loved him, and out of Egypt I called my son. But the more I called Israel, the further they went away from me. They sacrificed to the Baals, and they burned incense to images. It was I who taught Ephraim to walk, taking them by the arms, but

they did not realize it was I who healed them. I led them with the cords of human kindness, with ties of love. (Hosea 11:1–4)

As Jesus Christ pointed out in the Sermon on the Mount (Matthew 7:9–11), even human fathers want to give their children good things. So how much more will God, as our heavenly father, want to give good things to those who ask for them in prayer?

It is the fourth aspect of this analogy which has generated most heat, and which needs further discussion. Both the Old and New Testaments use male language about God. The Greek word for "god" (*theos*) is unquestionably masculine, and most of the analogies used for God throughout scripture – such as father, king, and shepherd – are male. Does this mean that God *is* male?

It is important to note that the Bible also uses female imagery to refer to the love of God for humanity. Just as a mother can never forget or turn against her child, so God will not forget or turn against his people (Isaiah 49:15). There is a natural bond of affection and sympathy between God and his children, simply because he has brought them into being. Thus, God loved us long before we loved God (1 John 4:10, 19). Psalm 51:1 refers to God's "great compassion." It is interesting to note that the Hebrew word for "compassion" (*rachmin*) is derived from the word for "womb" (*rechmen*). God's compassion towards his people is that of a mother towards her child (cf. Isaiah 66:12–13). Compassion stems from the womb.

So is God male? Does speaking of God as "father" mean that Christianity believes in a male deity? Earlier, we noted the analogical nature of theological language. Individual persons or social roles, largely drawn from the rural world of the ancient Near East, are identified as models for the divine activity or personality. One such analogy is that of a shepherd; another is that of a father. Yet the statement that "a father in ancient Israelite society is a suitable analogy for God" is not equivalent to saying that "God is male." To speak of God as father is to say that the role of the father in ancient Israel allows us insights into the nature of God. It is not to say that God *is* a male human being. Yet the Old Testament is clear that mothers were also analogies for aspects of God's love for Israel. Although there are many more references to paternal role models than to maternal, there is no doubt that both fathers and mothers function as analogies for God in the Bible.

The important point to appreciate here is that *neither* male nor female sexuality is to be attributed to God. For sexuality is an attribute of the created order, which cannot be assumed to correspond directly to any such polarity within the creator God. Indeed, the Old Testament completely avoids attributing sexual functions to God, on account of the strongly pagan overtones of such associations. The Canaanite fertility cults emphasized the sexual functions of both gods and goddesses; the Old Testament refuses to endorse the idea that the gender or the sexuality of God is a significant matter.

The important German Lutheran theologian Wolfhart Pannenberg develops this point in his *Systematic Theology* (1990):

> The aspect of fatherly care in particular is taken over in what the Old Testament has to say about God's fatherly care for Israel. The sexual definition of the father's role plays no part . . . To bring sexual differentiation into the understanding of God would mean polytheism; it was thus ruled out for the God of Israel . . . The fact that God's care for Israel can also be expressed in terms of a mother's love shows clearly enough how little there is any sense of sexual distinction in the understanding of God as Father.

In an attempt to bring out the fact that God is not male, a number of recent writers have explored the idea of God as "mother" (which brings out the female aspects of God), or as "friend" (which brings out the more gender-neutral aspects of God). An excellent example of this is provided by the American theologian Sallie McFague, in her *Models of God*. Recognizing that speaking of "God as father" does not mean that God is male, she writes:

> God as mother does not mean that God is mother (or father). We imagine God as both mother and father, but we realize how

inadequate these and any other metaphors are to express the creative love of God . . . Nevertheless, we speak of this love in language that is familiar and dear to us, the language of mothers and fathers who give us life, from whose bodies we come, and upon whose care we depend.

The new interest in the issues raised by the maleness of most of the biblical images of God has led to a careful reading of the spiritual literature of early periods in Christian history, resulting in an increased appreciation of the use of female imagery during these earlier periods. An excellent example of this is provided by the *Revelations of Divine Love,* an account of sixteen visions which appeared to the English writer Julian of Norwich in May 1373. The visions are notable for their distinctive tendency to refer to both God and Jesus Christ in strongly maternal terms:

I saw that God rejoices to be our Father, and also that he rejoices to be our Mother; and yet again, that he rejoices to be our true Husband, with our soul as his beloved bride . . . He is the foundation, substance and the thing itself, what it is by nature. He is the true Father and Mother of what things are by nature.

Talking about God as "shepherd" or "father" leads us on to another important theme of Christian thinking about God – namely, the concept of a *personal* God, to which we now turn.

A Personal God

Down the ages, theologians and ordinary Christian believers alike have had no hesitation in speaking about God in personal terms. For example, Christianity has ascribed to God a whole series of attributes, such as love, trustworthiness, and purpose, which seemed to have strongly personal associations. Many writers have pointed out that the Christian practice of prayer seems to be modeled on the relationship between a child and a parent. Prayer expresses a gracious relationship which "is simply trust in a person whose whole dealing with us proves him worthy of trust" (John Oman). Similarly, one of Paul's leading soteriological images – reconciliation – is clearly modeled on human personal relationships ("soteriology" means "making sense of salvation"). It implies that the transformation through faith of the relationship between God and sinful human beings is like the reconciliation of two persons, such as an alienated husband and wife.

For early Christian writers, the word "person" is an expression of the individuality of a human being, as seen in his or her words and actions. Above all, there is an emphasis upon the idea of social relationships. A person is someone who plays a role in a social drama, who relates to others. A person has a part to play within a network of social relationships. "Individuality" does not imply social relationships, whereas "personality" relates to the part played by an individual in a web of relationships, by which that person is perceived to be distinctive by others. The basic idea expressed by the idea of a "personal God" is thus a God with whom we can exist in a relationship which is analogous to that which we could have with another human person.

It is helpful to consider what overtones the phrase an "impersonal God" would convey. The phrase suggests a God who is distant or aloof, who deals with humanity (if God deals with us at all) in general terms which take no account of human individuality. The idea of a personal relationship, such as love, suggests a reciprocal character to God's dealings with us. This idea is incorporated into the notion of a personal God, but not into impersonal conceptions of the nature of God. There are strongly negative overtones to the idea of "impersonal," which have passed into Christian thinking about the nature of God.

It is also important to appreciate that personal relationships establish the framework within which such key biblical themes as love, trust, and faithfulness have their meaning. Both the Old and New Testaments are full of statements concerning the "love of God," the "trustworthiness of God," and the "faithfulness of God." "Love" is a word which is used primarily of personal relationships. Furthermore, the great biblical theme of promise and fulfillment is ultimately based upon a personal relationship, in that God promises certain quite definite things (such as eternal life and forgiveness) to certain individuals. One of the great themes which dominates the Old Testament in particular is that of the covenant between God and people, by which they mutually bind themselves to each other. "I will be their God, and they will be my people" (Jeremiah 31:33). The basic idea underlying this is the personal commitment of God to God's people, and of God's people to their God.

A twentieth-century philosophical analysis of what it means to speak of a "person" is also helpful in clarifying what it means to speak of a personal God. In his major work *I and Thou* (1927), the Jewish writer Martin Buber drew a fundamental distinction between two categories of relations: *I-Thou* relations, which are "personal," and *I-It* relations, which are impersonal. We shall explore these basic distinctions further, before considering their theological importance.

1   *I-It relations:* Buber uses this category to refer to the relation between subjects and objects; for example, between a human being and a pencil. The human being is active, whereas the pencil is passive. This distinction is often referred to in more philosophical language as a *subject-object relation*, in which an active subject (in this case, the human being) relates to an inactive object (in this case, the pencil). According to Buber, the subject acts as an *I*, and the object as an *It*. The relation between the human being and pencil could thus be described as an *I-It* relation.

2   *I-Thou relations:* At this point, we come to the heart of Buber's philosophy. An I-Thou relation exists between two active subjects, between two *persons*. It is something which is *mutual* and *reciprocal*. "The I of the primary word I-Thou makes its appearance as a person, and becomes conscious of itself." In other words, Buber is suggesting that human personal relationships exemplify the essential features of an I-You relation. It is the relationship itself, that intangible and invisible bond which links two persons, which is the heart of Buber's idea of an I-Thou relation.

What, then, are the theological implications of this approach to personhood? How does Buber's philosophy help us to understand and explore the idea of God as a person? A number of key ideas emerge, all of which have important and helpful theological applications. Furthermore, Buber anticipated some of these himself. In the final sections of *I and Thou*, he explores the implications of his approach to thinking and speaking about God, or to use his preferred term, the "Absolute Thou."

1   Buber's approach affirms that God cannot be reduced to a concept, or to some neat conceptual formulation. According to Buber, only an "It" can be treated in this way. For Buber, God is the "Thou who can, by its nature, never become an It. That is, God is a being who escapes all attempts at objectification and transcends all description." Theology must learn to acknowledge and wrestle with the presence of God, realizing that this presence cannot be reduced to a neat package of contents.

2   The approach allows valuable insights into the idea of revelation. For Christian theology, God's revelation is not simply a making known of facts about God, but a self-revelation of God. Revelation of ideas about God is to be supplemented by revelation of God as a person, a presence as much as a content. We could make sense of this by saying that revelation includes knowledge of God as an "It" and as a "Thou." We come to know things about God; yet we also come to know God. Similarly, "knowledge of God" includes knowledge of God as both "It" and "Thou." "Knowing God" is not simply a collection of data about God, but a personal relationship.

3   Buber's "dialogical personalism" also avoids the idea of God as an object, perhaps the weakest and most heavily criticized aspect of some nineteenth-century liberal Protestant theology. The characteristic non-inclusive nineteenth-century phrase "man's quest for God" summed up the basic premise of this approach: God is an "It," a passive object, waiting to be discovered by (male) theologians, who are viewed as active subjects. Writers such as Emil Brunner in his *Truth as*

Encounter, argued that God had to be viewed as a Thou, an active subject. As such, God could take the initiative away from humans, through self-revelation and a willingness to be known in a historical and personal form; namely, Jesus Christ. Theology would thus become the human response to God's self-disclosure, rather than the human quest for God.

God as Almighty

The Apostles' Creed, however, goes on to speak of God as "almighty." So what do we mean when we say that God is "almighty" in this way? At first sight, this might seem to be rather pointless. The meaning of the word "almighty" is perfectly obvious in everyday language. It means "capable of doing anything." And as we believe that God is indeed almighty, we are simply saying that God can do anything. This would appear to bring discussion of the matter to an end. What more is there to say?

Yet one of the tasks of theology is to encourage us to use language critically – to make us think about what we really mean when we talk about God. Is it really quite as simple as this? Might not the word "almighty" have a subtle difference when applied to God than when applied to a human? To explore this, let's consider a simple statement:

> *"To say that God is almighty means that God can do anything."*

If you are in a study group, you might like to discuss this statement. If you are working on your own, pause at this point, and think about it. Is it right? What issues does it raise? At first, it seems fairly straightforward. Yet it runs into some difficulties at an early stage. Consider the following question: "Can God draw a triangle with four sides?" It does not take much thought to see that this question has to be answered in the negative. Triangles have three sides; to draw something with four sides is to draw a quadrilateral, not a triangle.

Now we may turn to another question: "Can God create a stone which is too heavy for God to lift?" This question involves a nice logical puzzle. If God cannot create such a stone, there is something that God cannot do. Yet if God can create such a stone, then God will not be able to lift it – and so there is something else God cannot do. Whatever way the question is answered, God's ability to do anything is called into question. In other words, God's omnipotence is called into question in each situation.

However, on further reflection, it is not clear that these questions cause problems for the Christian understanding of God. Four-sided triangles do not and cannot exist. The fact that God cannot make such a triangle is not a serious issue. It just forces us to restate our simple statement in a more complicated way: "To say that God is almighty means that God can do anything that does not involve logical contradiction." Or we can follow Thomas Aquinas, who remarked that it was not that God could not do such things; it was simply that such things cannot be done.

Yet theology is about rather more than such logical riddles. The real issue concerns the divine nature itself. We can begin to engage with this important matter by considering a question beloved of medieval philosophers:

"Can God make someone who loves him hate him?"

Again, you might like to pause at this point, and think about this, perhaps discussing it in a group. At first sight, the question seems a little strange. Why should God want to turn someone's love for him into a hatred? The question appears unreal and pointless. On closer examination, however, the question begins to make sense. At one level, there is no problem. "To say that God is almighty means that God can do anything that does not involve logical contradiction." There is clearly no such contradiction here. God must have the ability to turn someone's love into hatred. Yet there is obviously a deeper issue here, concerning the *character* of God. Can we ever imagine God *wanting* to do this?

To make this important point clearer, let us ask another question. "Can God break promises?" There is no logical contradiction involved in breaking promises. It happens all the time. It may be regrettable, but there is no intellectual difficulty here. If God can do anything that does not involve a logical contradiction, God can certainly break a promise.

Yet, for Christians, this suggestion is outrageous. The God who we know and love is one who remains faithful to what has been promised. If we cannot trust God, whom can we trust? The suggestion that God might break a promise contradicts a vital aspect of God's character – namely, God's faithfulness and truthfulness. One of the great themes of the Old and New Testaments is the total trustworthiness and reliability of God. Humans may fail; God remains faithful. Consider these biblical verses:

> Know therefore that the LORD your God is God. He is the faithful God, keeping his covenant of love to a thousand generations. (Deuteronomy 7:9)

> The LORD is faithful to all his promises. (Psalm 145:13)

The point here is that there is a tension between power and trust. An all-powerful cheater can make promises which cannot be relied upon. Yet one of the greatest insights of the Christian faith is that we know a God who *could* do anything – but who *chose* to redeem us. God did not need to enter into a covenant with Israel – but God chose to do so, and having done so, remains faithful to this promise. We see here the important idea of divine self-limitation – the notion that God freely chooses to behave in certain ways, and in doing so, places limits on divine action. God cannot be accused of acting arbitrarily or whimsically; rather, God acts reliably and faithfully.

If God is indeed revealed in Christ, we must realize that God's power is not symbolized by the sword or the chariot – common symbols of military and political might in the world of Jesus' day – but by the cross, a symbol associated with shame, defeat, and *powerlessness*. Perhaps the most dramatic statement of this notion of divine self-limitation can be found in Dietrich Bonhoeffer's

Letters and Papers from Prison, dating from the closing years of World War II:

> God lets himself be pushed out of the world on to the cross. He is weak and powerless in the world, and that is precisely the way, the only way, in which he is with us and helps us . . . The Bible directs us to God's powerlessness and suffering; only the suffering God can help.

In an age which has become increasingly suspicious of the idea of "power," it is important to be reminded that talk about "an almighty God" does not imply that God is a tyrant. For Bonhoeffer, it means that God chooses to stand alongside people in their powerlessness – a major theme in interpretations of the cross of Christ, to which we shall return shortly.

But let us return to the question with which we began. Can God do anything? The commonsense answer would be simple and straightforward. If God is almighty, God must be capable of doing anything. Yet Christian theology insists that God's omnipotence is to be set within the context of God's nature – that of a righteous and faithful God, whose promises are to be trusted. As proves so often to be the case, we must be very careful in transferring concepts from their human contexts when we use them to refer to God.

Engaging with a Text

The *Catechism of the Catholic Church* is one of the most important theological documents of the twentieth century, and has won much admiration for its clarity of presentation. In its discussion of what it means to refer to God as "father," the *Catechism* brings together a number of important points, all of which are worth careful consideration. Here is the text:

> By calling God "Father," the language of faith indicates two main things: that God is the first origin of everything and transcendent

authority; and that he is at the same time goodness and loving care for all his children. God's parental tenderness can also be expressed by the image of motherhood, which emphasizes God's immanence, the intimacy between Creator and creature. The language of faith thus draws on the human experience of parents, who are in a way the first representatives of God for man. But this experience also tells us that human parents are fallible and can disfigure the face of fatherhood and motherhood. We ought therefore to recall that God transcends the human distinction between the sexes. He is neither man nor woman: he is God. He also transcends human fatherhood and motherhood, although he is their origin and standard: no one is father as God is Father.

You may find the following framework helpful as you interact with this text, on your own or within a discussion group.

1   What are the two main points that the *Catechism* believes are made through using the image of God as father? You might like to try and identify some biblical passages which underlie these.

2   The *Catechism* also stresses the importance of maternal imagery. In what ways does this supplement the paternal imagery? And how are these themes held together by an appeal to the "parental" love of God?

3   What do you think the *Catechism* means when it says that "no one is father as God is Father"?

CHAPTER 3

Creation

All Christian creeds emphasize that God is the creator of the world. This theme is found throughout the Christian Bible, and is the first theme that we encounter when reading the Bible in its canonical order – in other words, when beginning with the book of Genesis (a Greek word, which literally means "beginning" or "origin"). It is therefore appropriate to begin this chapter by exploring the Old Testament's understanding of creation.

Creation in the Old Testament

The theme of "God as creator" is of major importance within the Old Testament. Attention has often focused on the creation narratives found in the first two chapters of the Book of Genesis, with which the Old Testament opens. However, it must be appreciated that the theme is deeply embedded in the wisdom and prophetic literature in the Old Testament. For example, Job 38:1–42:6 sets out what is unquestionably the most comprehensive understanding of God as creator to be found in the Old Testament, stressing the role of God as creator and sustainer of the world.

It is possible to discern two distinct, though related, contexts in which the notion of "God as creator" is encountered: first, in contexts which reflect the praise of God within Israel's worship, both individual and corporate; and secondly, in contexts which stress that the God who created the world is also the God who liberated Israel from bondage, and continues to sustain her in the present.

Of particular interest for our purposes is the Old Testament theme of "creation as ordering," and the manner in which the critically important theme of "order" is established on – and justified with reference to – cosmological foundations. It has often been pointed out how the Old Testament portrays creation in terms of an engagement with and victory over forces of chaos. This "establishment of order" is generally represented in two different ways:

1   Creation is an imposition of order on a formless chaos. This model is especially associated with the image of a potter working clay into a recognizably ordered structure (e.g., Genesis 2:7; Isaiah 29:16; 44:8; Jeremiah 18:1–6).
2   Creation concerns conflict with a series of chaotic forces, often depicted as a dragon or another monster (variously named "Behemoth," "Leviathan," "Nahar," "Rahab," "Tannim," or "Yam") who must be subdued (Job 3:8; 7:12; 9:13; 40:15–32; Psalms 74:13–15; 139:10–11; Isaiah 27:1; 41:9–10; Zechariah 10:11).

It is clear that there are parallels between the Old Testament account of God engaging with the forces of chaos and similar accounts found in other religious texts of the Ancient Near East (for example, Ugaritic and Canaanite mythology). Nevertheless, there are significant differences at points of importance, not least in the Old Testament's insistence that the forces of chaos are not to be seen as divine. Creation is not to be understood simply as the forming of the universe, but in terms of God's mastery of chaos and ordering of the world.

Perhaps one of the most significant affirmations which the Old Testament makes is that *nature is not divine*. The Genesis creation account stresses that God created the moon, sun, and stars. The significance of this point is too easily overlooked. Each of these celestial entities was worshipped as divine in the ancient world. By asserting that they were created by God, the Old Testament is insisting that they are subordinate to God, and have no intrinsic divine nature.

The Concept of Creation *ex nihilo*

Having briefly introduced some aspects of the concept of creation, we may now pass on to consider some of its aspects in a more theological manner. One of the most important developments of the doctrine of creation arose in response to the Gnostic controversy of the second century. For Gnosticism, in most of its significant forms, a sharp distinction was to be drawn between the God who redeemed humanity from the world, and a somewhat inferior deity (often termed "the demiurge") who created that world in the first place. The Old Testament was regarded by the Gnostics as dealing with this lesser deity, whereas the New Testament was concerned with the redeemer God. As such, belief in God as creator and in the authority of the Old Testament came to be interlinked at an early stage. Of the early writers to deal with this theme, Irenaeus of Lyons is of particular importance.

A distinct debate centered on the question of creation *ex nihilo* ("out of nothing"). It must be remembered that Christianity initially took root and then expanded in the Eastern Mediterranean world of the first and second centuries, which was dominated by various Greek philosophies. The general Greek understanding of the origins of the world could be summarized as follows. God is not to be thought of as having *created* the world. Rather, God is to be thought of as an architect, who ordered preexistent matter. Matter was already present within the universe, and did not require to be created; it needed to be given a definite shape and structure. God was therefore thought of as the one who fashioned the world from this already existing matter. Thus, in one of his dialogues (*Timaeus*), Plato developed the idea that the world was made out of preexistent matter, which was fashioned into the present form of the world.

This idea was taken up by most Gnostic writers, who were here followed by individual Christian theologians such as Theophilus of Antioch and Justin Martyr. They professed a belief in preexistent matter, which was shaped into the world in the act of creation. In other words, creation was not *ex nihilo*; rather, it was to be seen as an act of construction, on the basis of material which was already to hand, as one might construct an igloo out of snow, or a house from stone. The existence of evil in the world was thus to be explained on the basis of the intractability of this preexistent matter. God's options in creating the world were limited by the poor quality of the material available. The presence of evil or defects within the world are thus not to be ascribed to God, but to deficiencies in the material from which the world was constructed.

However, the conflict with Gnosticism forced reconsideration of this issue. In part, the idea of creation from preexistent matter was discredited by its Gnostic associations; in part, it was called into question by an increasingly sophisticated reading of the Old Testament creation narratives. Reacting against this Platonist worldview, several major Christian writers of the second and third centuries argued that *everything* had to be created by God. There was no preexistent matter; everything required to be created out of nothing. Irenaeus argued that the Christian doctrine of creation affirmed the inherent goodness of creation, which contrasted sharply with the Gnostic idea that the material world was evil.

Tertullian (ca. 160–ca. 225) emphasized the divine decision to create the world. The existence of the world is itself due to God's freedom and goodness, not to any inherent necessity arising from the nature of matter. The world depends on God for its existence. This contrasted sharply with the Aristotelian view that the world depended on nothing for its existence, and that the particular structure of the world was intrinsically necessary. Yet not all Christian theologians adopted this position at this early stage in the emergence of the Christian tradition. Origen (ca. 185–ca. 254), perhaps one of the most Platonist of early Christian writers, clearly regarded the doctrine of creation from preexistent matter to have some merit.

The central issue relating to the doctrine of creation which had to be debated in the first period of Christian theology was thus that of *dualism*. The classic example of this is found in some of the forms of Gnosticism, so forcefully opposed by Irenaeus, which argued for the existence of two gods – a supreme god, who was the source of the invisible spiritual world, and a lesser deity who created the world of material things. This approach is strongly dualist, in that it sets up fundamental tension between the spiritual realm (which is seen as being good) and the material realm (which is seen as being evil). The doctrine of creation affirmed that the material world was created good by God, despite its subsequent contamination by sin. A similar outlook is associated with Manichaeism, a Gnostic worldview which Augustine found attractive as a young man.

By the end of the fourth century, most Christian theologians had rejected the Platonist approach, even in the form associated with Origen, and argued for God being the creator of both the spiritual and material worlds. The Nicene Creed opens with a declaration of faith in God as "maker of heaven and earth," thus affirming the divine creation of both the spiritual and material realms. During the Middle Ages, forms of dualism once more made their appearance, particularly in the views of the Cathari and Albigenses, who taught that matter is evil, and was created *ex nihilo* by the devil. Against such views, the Fourth Lateran Council (1215) and the Council of Florence (1442) taught explicitly that God created a good creation out of nothing.

Implications of the Doctrine of Creation

The doctrine of God as creator has several major implications, of which four may be noted here.

First, a distinction must be drawn between God and the creation. A major theme of Christian theology from the earliest of times has been to resist the temptation to merge the creator and the creation. The theme is clearly stated in Paul's Letter to the Romans, the opening chapter of which criticizes the tendency to reduce God to the level of the world. According to Paul, there is a natural human tendency, as a result of sin, to serve "created things rather than the creator" (Romans 1:25). A central task of a Christian theology of creation is to distinguish God from the creation, while at the same time to affirm that it is *God's* creation.

This process may be seen at work in the writings of Augustine. It is also of considerable importance in the writings of reformers such as Calvin, who were concerned to forge a world-affirming spirituality in response to the general monastic tendency to renounce the world, evident in writings such as Thomas à Kempis' *Imitation of Christ*, with its characteristic emphasis upon the "contempt of the world." There is a tension in Calvin's thought between the world as the creation of God himself, and the world as the fallen creation. In that it is God's creation, it is to be honored, respected, and affirmed; in that it is a fallen creation, it is to be criticized with the object of redeeming it. These two insights could be described as the twin foci of the ellipse of Calvin's world-affirming spirituality. A similar pattern can be discerned in Calvin's doctrine of human nature, where – despite his stress upon the sinful nature of fallen humanity – he never loses sight of the fact that it remains God's creation. Though stained by sin, it remains the creation and possession of God, and is to be valued for that reason. The doctrine of creation thus leads to a critical world-affirming spirituality, in which the world is affirmed, without falling into the snare of treating it as if it were God.

In the second place, creation implies God's authority over the world. A characteristic biblical emphasis is that the creator has authority over the creation. Humans are thus regarded as part of that creation, with special functions within it. The doctrine of creation leads to the idea of *human stewardship of the creation*, which is to be contrasted with a secular notion of *human owner-ship of the world*. The creation is not ours; we hold it in trust for God. We are meant to be the stewards of God's creation, and are responsible for the manner in which we exercise that stewardship. This insight is of major importance in relation to ecological and environmental concerns, in that it provides a theoretical foundation for the exercise of human responsibility toward the planet.

In the third place, the doctrine of God as creator implies the goodness of creation. Throughout the first biblical account of creation, we encounter the affirmation: "And God saw that it was good" (Genesis 1:10, 18, 21, 25, 31). (The only thing, inciden-tally, that is "not good" is that Adam is alone. Humanity is created as a social being, and is meant to exist in relation with others.) There is no place in Christian theology for the Gnostic or dualist idea of the world as an inherently evil place. As we shall explore elsewhere, even though the world is fallen through sin, it remains God's good creation, and capable of being redeemed.

This is not to say that the creation is presently perfect. An essential component of the Christian doctrine of sin is the recog-nition that the world has departed from the trajectory upon which God placed it in the work of creation. It has become deflected from its intended course. It has fallen from the glory in which it was created. The world as we see it is not the world as it was intended to be. The existence of human sin, evil, and death are themselves tokens of the extent of the departure of the created order from its intended pattern. For this reason, most Christian reflections on redemption include the idea of some kind of restoration of creation to its original integrity, in order that God's intentions for his creation might find fulfillment. Affirming the goodness of creation also avoids the suggestion, unacceptable to most theologians, that God is responsible for evil. The constant biblical emphasis upon the goodness of creation is a reminder that the destructive force of sin is not present in the world by God's design or permission.

In the fourth place, the doctrine of creation affirms that human beings are created in the image of God (Genesis 1:26–7). This insight, central to any Christian doctrine of human nature, is of major importance as an aspect of the doctrine of creation itself. "You made us for yourself, and our hearts are restless until they find their rest in you" (Augustine of Hippo). With these words, the importance of the doctrine of creation for a proper understanding of human experience, nature, and destiny is established.

Models of God as Creator

The manner in which God acts as creator has been the subject of intense discussion within the Christian tradition. A number of models of, or ways of picturing, the manner in which God is to be thought of as creating the world have been developed, each of which casts some light on the complex and rich Christian understanding of the notion of creation.

Emanation

This term was widely used by early Christian writers to clarify the relation between God and the world. Although the term is not used by either Plato or Plotinus, many patristic writers sympathetic to the various forms of Platonism saw it as a convenient and appropriate way of articulating Platonic insights. The image that dominates this approach is that of light or heat radiating from the sun, or a human source such as a fire. This image of creation (hinted at in the Nicene Creed's phrase "light from light") suggests that the creation of the world can be regarded as an overflowing of the creative energy of God. Just as light derives from the sun and reflects its nature, so the created order derives from God, and expresses the divine nature. There is, on the basis of this model, a *natural* or *organic* connection between God and the creation.

However, the model has weaknesses, of which two may be noted. First, the image of a sun radiating light, or a fire radiating heat, implies an involuntary emanation, rather than a conscious decision to create. The Christian tradition has consistently emphasized that the act of creation rests upon a prior decision on the part of God to create, which this model cannot adequately express.

This naturally leads on to the second weakness, which relates to the impersonal nature of the model in question. The idea of a personal God, expressing a personality both in the very act of creation and the subsequent creation itself, is difficult to convey by this image. Nevertheless, the model clearly articulates a close connection between creator and creation, leading us to expect that something of the identity and nature of the creator is to be found in the creation. Thus, the beauty of God – a theme which was of particular importance in early medieval theology, and has emerged as significant again in the later writings of Hans Urs von Balthasar – would be expected to be reflected in the nature of the creation.

Construction

Many biblical passages portray God as a master builder, deliberately constructing the world (for example, Psalm 127:1). The imagery is powerful, conveying the ideas of purpose, planning, and a deliberate intention to create. The image is important, in that it draws attention to both the creator and the creation. In addition to bringing out the skill of the creator, it also allows the beauty and ordering of the resulting creation to be appreciated, both for what it is in itself, and for its testimony to the creativity and care of its creator.

However, the image has a deficiency, which relates to a point we made in connection with Plato's dialogue *Timaeus*. This portrays creation as involving preexistent matter. Here, creation is understood as giving shape and form to something which is already there – an idea which, we have seen, causes at least a degree of tension with the doctrine of creation *ex nihilo*. The image of God as a builder would seem to imply the assembly of the world from material which is already to hand, which is clearly deficient.

Nevertheless, despite this difficulty, it can be seen that the model expresses the insight that the character of the creator is, in some manner, expressed in the natural world, just as that of an artist is communicated or embodied in her work. In particular, the notion of "ordering" – that is, the imparting or imposing of a coherence or structure to the material in question – is clearly affirmed by this model. Whatever else the complex notion of creation may mean within a Christian context, it certainly includes the fundamental theme of ordering – a notion which is especially significant in the creation narratives of the Old Testament.

Artistic expression

Many Christian writers, from various periods in the history of the church, speak of creation as the "handiwork of God," comparing it to a work of art which is both beautiful in itself, as well as expressing the personality of its creator. This model of creation as the "artistic expression" of God as creator is particularly well described in the writings of the eighteenth-century North American theologian Jonathan Edwards, who had a particular interest in the beauty of nature.

The image is profoundly helpful, in that it supplements a deficiency of both the models noted above – namely, their impersonal character. The image of God as artist conveys the idea of personal expression in the creation of something beautiful. Once more, the potential weaknesses need to be noted: for example, the model could easily lead to the idea of creation from pre-existent matter, as in the case of a sculptor with a statue carved from an already existing block of stone. However, the model offers us at least the possibility of thinking about creation from nothing, as with the author who writes a novel, or the composer who creates a melody and harmony. It also encourages us to seek for the self-expression of God in the creation, and gives added theological credibility to a natural theology. There is also a natural link between the concept of creation as artistic expression and the highly significant concept of beauty.

Creation and Natural Theology

So if God created the world, what may be known of God from the world? This question has been debated within Christian theology for centuries. "The heavens declare the glory of God; the heavens proclaim the work of God's hands" (Psalm 19:1). This well-known text can be seen as representing a general theme within the Christian Bible – that something of the wisdom of the God who made the world can be known through the world that was created. The exploration of this theme has proved to be one of the most fruitful areas of theology. We begin our discussion by considering what is widely regarded as a landmark in this matter: the contribution of Thomas Aquinas.

Thomas Aquinas' *Summa contra Gentiles* was written during the period 1259–61, initially at Paris and subsequently at Naples. One of its most significant discussions concerns the manner in which God may be understood to be related to the creation – a relationship which Aquinas analyses in terms of causality, as follows.

For Aquinas, there exists a fundamental "likeness (*similitudo*) to God" within the created order as a consequence of God being the cause, in some sense of the word, of all created things. In that no created thing can be said to come into existence spontaneously, the existence of all things can be considered to be a consequence of a relationship of causal dependence between the creation and its creator. Using what are essentially Aristotelian categories of causality, Aquinas sets out a position which we may summarize as follows:

1   Suppose that A causes B.
2   Suppose also that A possesses a quality Q.
3   Then B will also possess that quality Q as a result of its being caused by A.

The full argument set out by Aquinas is complex, and not without its difficulties; nevertheless, its conclusion is clear. There are, so to speak, physical or metaphysical fingerprints within creation, which provide the basis for an inductive argument to the existence of its cause and origins.

If God made the world, God's "signature" (so to speak) may be found within the created order. Thomas Aquinas puts this point as follows:

> Meditation on [God's] works enables us, at least to some extent, to admire and reflect on God's wisdom . . . We are thus able to infer God's wisdom from reflection upon God's works . . . This consideration of God's works leads to an admiration of God's sublime power, and consequently inspires reverence for God in human hearts . . . This consideration also incites human souls to the love of God's goodness . . . If the goodness, beauty and wonder of creatures are so delightful to the human mind, the fountainhead of God's own goodness (compared with the trickles of goodness found in creatures) will draw excited human minds entirely to itself.

Something of the torrent of God's beauty can thus be known in the rivulets of the beauty of the creation.

Another theologian to explore this issue is John Calvin. The first book of Calvin's *Institutes* opens with discussion of this fundamental problem of Christian theology: how do we know anything about God? Calvin affirms that a general knowledge of God may be discerned throughout the creation – in humanity, in the natural order, and in the historical process itself. Two main grounds of such knowledge are identified, one subjective, the other objective.

The first ground is a "sense of divinity" (*sensus divinitatis*) or a "seed of religion" (*semen religionis*), which has been planted within every human being by God. God has endowed human beings with some inbuilt sense or presentiment of the divine existence. It is as if something about God has been engraved in the heart of every human being. Calvin identifies three consequences of this inbuilt awareness of divinity: the universality of religion (which, if uninformed by the Christian revelation, degenerates into idolatry), a troubled conscience, and a servile fear of God. All of these, Calvin suggests, may serve as points of contact for the Christian proclamation.

The second ground of knowledge of God as creator lies in experience of and reflection upon the ordering of the world. The fact that God is creator, together with an appreciation of the divine wisdom and justice, may be gained from an inspection of the created order, culminating in humanity itself.

It is important to stress that Calvin makes no suggestion whatsoever that this knowledge of God from the created order is peculiar to, or even restricted to, Christian believers. Calvin is arguing that *anyone*, by intelligent and rational reflection upon the created order, should be able to arrive at the idea of God. The created order is a "theater" or a "mirror" for the displaying of the divine presence, nature, and attributes. Although invisible and incomprehensible, God wills to be known under the form of created and visible things within creation. The creator God can be known, although to a limited extent, through the creation itself.

Calvin then introduces the notion of revelation. Scripture reiterates what may be known of God through nature, while simultaneously clarifying this general revelation and enhancing it. "The knowledge of God, which is clearly shown in the ordering of the world and in all creatures, is still more clearly and familiarly explained in the Word." It is only through scripture that the believer has access to knowledge of the redeeming actions of God in history, culminating in the life, death, and resurrection of Jesus Christ. For Calvin, revelation is focused upon the person of Jesus Christ; our knowledge of God is mediated through him. God may thus be fully known only through Jesus Christ, who may in turn be known only through scripture.

However, the created order provides important points of contact for this revelation.

The basic idea is that a knowledge of God the creator may be had both through nature and through revelation, with the latter clarifying, confirming, and extending what may be known through the former. Knowledge of God the redeemer – which, for Calvin, is a distinctively *Christian* knowledge of God – may only be had by the Christian revelation, in Christ and through scripture.

Yet not all theologians are persuaded of the merits and legitimacy of natural theology. Perhaps the most negative attitude to have been adopted in recent Christian theology is that of Karl Barth, whose 1934 controversy with Emil Brunner over this issue has become a landmark in theological debate. In 1934 Brunner published a work entitled *Nature and Grace*. In this work he argued that "the task of our theological generation is to find a way back to a legitimate natural theology." Brunner located this approach in the doctrine of creation, specifically the idea that human beings are created in the *imago Dei*, the "image of God." Human nature is constituted in such a way that there is an analog with the being of God. Despite the sinfulness of human nature, the ability to discern God in nature remains. Sinful human beings remain able to recognize God in nature and in the events of history, and to be aware of their guilt before God. There is thus a "point of contact" for divine revelation within human nature as a consequence of the doctrine of creation.

Brunner argued that human nature is constituted in such a way that there is a ready-made point of contact for divine revelation. Revelation thus addresses itself to a human nature which already has some idea of what that revelation is about. For example, take the gospel demand to "repent of sin." Brunner argues that this makes little sense, unless human beings already have some idea of what "sin" is. The gospel demand to repent is thus addressed to an audience which already has at least something of an idea of what "sin" and "repentance" might mean. Revelation brings with it a fuller understanding of what sin means – but in doing so, it builds upon an existing human awareness of sin.

Barth reacted with anger to this suggestion. His published reply to Brunner – which brought their long-standing friendship to an abrupt end – has one of the shortest titles in the history of religious publishing: *Nein!* ("No!") Barth was determined to say "no!" to Brunner's positive evaluation of natural theology. It seemed to imply that God needed help to become known, or that human beings somehow cooperated with God in the act of revelation. For Barth, this subverted God's freedom and sovereignty in revelation. "The Holy Spirit . . . needs no point of contact other than that which that same Spirit establishes," was his angry retort. For Barth, there was no "point of contact" inherent within human nature. Any such "point of contact" was itself the result of divine revelation. It is something that is evoked by the Word of God, rather than something which is a permanent feature of human nature.

Underlying this exchange is another matter, which is too easily overlooked. The Barth–Brunner debate took place in 1934, the year in which Adolf Hitler gained power in Germany. Underlying Brunner's appeal to nature is an idea, which can be traced back to Luther, known as "the orders of creation." According to Luther, God providentially established certain "orders" within creation, in order to prevent it collapsing into chaos. Those orders included the family, the church, and the state. (The close alliance between the church and the state in German Lutheran thought can be seen as reflecting this idea.) Nineteenth-century German liberal Protestantism had absorbed this idea, and developed a theology which allowed German culture, including a positive assessment of the state, to become of major importance theologically. Part of Barth's concern was that Brunner, perhaps unwittingly, had laid a theological foundation for allowing the state to become a model for God. And who, he wondered, wanted to model God on Adolf Hitler?

Others, however, have wondered about the accuracy of this criticism. Does the belief that God can be known to some limited extent really imply that we construct God in the image of Hitler? Critics of Barth, such as James Barr, argued that this was a remote possibility, which had been given undue credibility in Barth's writings on account of the political situation of his day. Yet it seemed to Barr to be a *remote* possibility. Rightly understood, natural theology had little, if anything, to do with the political situation in Nazi Germany. Yet Barth's critique of natural theology remains significant, despite this cautionary comment.

Engaging with a Text

Calvin's strong affirmation of a natural knowledge of God gave a significant stimulus to the development of the concept of natural theology within the confessional element of the Reformed tradition. Thus the Gallic Confession (1559) stated that God reveals himself to humanity in two manners:

> First, in his works, both in their creation and their preservation and control. Second, and more clearly, in his Word, which was revealed through oracles in the beginning, and which was subsequently committed to writing in the books which we call the Holy Scriptures.

A related idea was set out in the Belgic Confession (1561), which expanded the brief statement on natural theology found in the Gallic Confession. Once more, knowledge of God is affirmed to come about by two means: nature and scripture. The two themes which emerge clearly from these confessional statements can be summarized as follows:

1 There are two modes of knowing God, one through the natural order, and the second through scripture.
2 The second mode is clearer and fuller than the first.

In what follows, we shall examine the teaching on this issue set out in the second article of the Belgic Confession – or, to use its rather more fulsome title, "The Confession of Faith of the Reformed Walloon and Flemish Churches" – which was drawn up by Guido des Brès in 1561. The document is clearly dependent upon the earlier Gallic Confession, and can be seen as an expansion of its ideas at certain points.

> We know [God] in two manners. First, by the creation, preservation and government of the universe, which is before our eyes as a most beautiful book, in which all creatures, great and small, are like so many characters leading us to contemplate the invisible things of God, namely, his eternal power and Godhead, as the Apostle Paul declares (Romans 1:20). All of these things are sufficient to convince humanity, and leave them without excuse. Second, he makes himself known more clearly and fully to us by his holy and divine Word; that is to say, as far as is necessary for us to know in this life, to his glory and our salvation.

This brief statement proved to be of considerable importance to the development of both the biological and physical sciences in the Lowlands. The development of the microscope at the end of the seventeenth century by Anton Van Leeuwenhoek, a Dutch clockmaker, can be seen as an attempt to inspect the "little book" of nature in more detail, and hence to appreciate to a greater extent the wisdom of God in creation.

To help you interact with this text, either on your own or in group discussion, you might like to use the following framework.

1 Look up Romans 1.20, the text that plays such an important role in this document. Read it in its original context, beginning at verse 18. What point does Paul make? How is this developed within the Belgic Confession?
2 What understanding of the relation of natural and revealed knowledge of God is set out in the document itself? Do you think that this would encourage its readers to want to study nature in greater depth? If so, for what reasons?

CHAPTER 4

Jesus ✓

One of the most basic tasks of Christian theology is to clarify the identity and significance of Jesus Christ, the central figure of Christian faith. As even a cursory survey of the history of theology makes clear, Christians have always insisted that there was something special, something qualitatively different, about Jesus, which sets him apart from religious teachers or thinkers. But what is special about him? These questions are addressed in the area of Christian theology traditionally known as Christology. If theology is "trying to make sense of God," then Christology is "trying to make sense of Jesus Christ." A related term of importance should be noted here: "soteriology," remember, means "making sense of salvation."

Part of the task of Christian theology is to weave together the various elements of the biblical witness to the identity and significance of Jesus. The various biblical motifs that need to be integrated in this way include:

1 The terms that the New Testament uses to refer to Jesus.
2 What Jesus is understood to have achieved, which is understood to be directly related to his identity. There is a close link

between the Christian understanding of the *person* of Christ and the *work* of Christ. In other words, discussion of the *identity* of Christ is interlocked with discussion of the *achievement* of Christ. We shall explore this issue further when reflecting on salvation in the following chapter.

3   The impact that Jesus made upon people during his ministry – for example, through his healing.

4   The resurrection, which New Testament writers interpret as an endorsement and validation of Jesus' exalted status in regard to God. Thus, for Paul, the resurrection demonstrates that Jesus is the Son of God (Romans 1:3–4).

The limited space available for our discussion means that we cannot hope to explore all of these.

In view of the importance of the Bible to Christian theology, this chapter will focus on some biblical themes that need to be woven together to yield a full understanding of the identity of Jesus. We begin by reflecting on some titles used to refer to Jesus by New Testament writers, and their implications for his identity.

Messiah

The title "Christ," or "Messiah," is widely used to designate Jesus in the New Testament. These two words refer to the same idea, the former being the Greek version, the latter the Hebrew. (Both the Greek and Hebrew words are mentioned together in John 1:41). When Peter recognizes Jesus as "the Christ, the Son of the living God" (Matthew 16:16), he is identifying Jesus with the long-awaited Messiah. It is very easy for a modern Western reader to assume that "Christ" was Jesus' surname, and to fail to appreciate that it is actually a title: "Jesus the Christ."

The term "Messiah" literally means "the anointed one" – someone who has been anointed with oil. This Old Testament practice indicated that the person anointed in this way was regarded as having been singled out by God as having special powers and functions; thus 1 Samuel 24:6 refers to the king as "the Lord's anointed." The basic sense of the word could be said to be "the divinely appointed King of Israel." As time passed, the term gradually came to refer to a deliverer, himself a descendent of David, who would restore Israel to the golden age she enjoyed under the rule of David.

During the period of Jesus' life, Palestine was occupied and administered by Rome. There was fierce nationalist feeling at the time, fueled by intense resentment at the presence of a foreign occupying power, and this appears to have given a new force to the traditional expectation of the coming of the Messiah. For many, the Messiah would be the deliverer who expelled the Romans from Israel, and restored the line of David. It is clear that Jesus refused to see himself as Messiah in this sense. At no point in his ministry do we find any violence against Rome suggested or condoned, nor even an explicit attack on the Roman administration. Jesus' attacks are directed primarily against his own people. Thus, after his triumphal entry into Jerusalem (Matthew 21:8–11), which gives every indication of being a deliberate Messianic demonstration or gesture, Jesus immediately evicts the merchants from the Temple (Matthew 21:12–13).

Jesus does not appear to have been prepared to accept the title "Messiah" in the course of his ministry. Mark's gospel should be read carefully to note this point. When Peter acclaims Jesus as Messiah – "You are the Christ!" – Jesus immediately tells him to keep quiet about it (Mark 8:29–30). It is not clear what the full significance of the "Messianic secret" is. Why should Mark emphasize that Jesus did not make an explicit claim to be the Messiah, when he was so clearly regarded as such by so many?

Perhaps the answer may be found later in Mark's gospel, when he recounts the only point at which Jesus explicitly acknowledges his identity as the Messiah. When Jesus is led, as a prisoner, before the High Priest, he admits to being the Messiah (Mark 14:61–2). Once violent or political action of any sort is no longer possible, Jesus reveals his identity. He was indeed the deliverer of the people of God – but not, it would seem, in any political sense of the term. The misunderstandings associated with the term, particularly in radical Jewish nationalist circles, appear to have caused Jesus to play down the Messianic side of his mission.

Jews did not expect their Messiah to be executed as a common criminal. It is worth noting that, immediately after Peter acknowledges Jesus as the Messiah, Jesus begins to explain to his disciples that he must suffer, be rejected by his own people, and be killed (Mark 8:29–31) – hardly an auspicious end to a Messianic career. Paul made it clear to the Corinthian Christians that the very idea of "a crucified Messiah" (or "a crucified Christ") was scandalous to a Jew (1 Corinthians 1:23). From a very early stage, it is clear that Christians recognized a link between Jesus' Messiahship and the destiny of the mysterious "Suffering Servant":

> He was despised, and rejected . . . A man of sorrows, acquainted with grief . . . He was despised, and we esteemed him not. Surely he has borne our griefs and carried our sorrows, yet we esteemed him stricken, smitten by God, and afflicted. But he was wounded for our transgressions, he was bruised for our iniquities. Upon him was the chastisement that made us whole. And with his stripes we are healed . . . The Lord has laid upon him the iniquity of us all. (Isaiah 53:3–6.)

Lord

A second title which claims our attention is "Lord" (Greek: *kyrios*). The word is used in two main senses in the New Testament. It is used as a polite title of respect, particularly when addressing someone. Thus, when Martha speaks to Jesus, and addresses him as "Lord" (John 11:21), she is probably, although not necessarily, merely treating Jesus with proper respect.

Of infinitely greater importance, however, are the frequent passages in the New Testament in which Jesus is referred to as "the Lord." The confession that "Jesus is Lord" (Romans 10:9;

1 Corinthians 12:3) was clearly regarded by Paul as a statement of the essential feature of the gospel. Christians are those who "call upon the name of the Lord" (Romans 10:13; 1 Corinthians 1:2). But what is implied by this? It is clear that there was a tendency in first-century Palestinian Judaism to use the word "Lord" (Greek: *kyrios*; Aramaic: *mare*) to designate a divine being, or at the very least a figure who is decidedly more than just human, in addition to its function as a polite or honorific title. But of particular importance is the use of this Greek word *kyrios* to translate the cipher of four letters used to refer to God in the Old Testament (often referred to as the "Tetragrammaton," from the Greek words for "four" and "letters").

The Old Testament writers were reluctant to refer to God directly, apparently regarding this as compromising his transcendence. On occasions where it was necessary to make reference to God, they tended to use a "cipher" of four letters, sometimes transliterated into English as YHWH. This group of letters, which lies behind the King James Version references to God as "Jehovah," and the Jerusalem Bible's references to God as "Yahweh," was used to represent the sacred name of God. Other Hebrew words could be used to refer to gods in general; this name was used to refer only to the "God of Abraham, Isaac and Jacob." It is specific to God, almost acting as a proper name. It is never used to refer to any other divine or angelic being, unlike other Hebrew words for "god." These latter words act as common nouns, referring to "god" or "gods" in general, and can be used to refer to Israel's own God, or to other gods (such as the pagan gods of other nations). But the Tetragrammaton is used only to name the specific God which Israel knew and worshipped, and who is made known through the life, death, and resurrection of Jesus Christ.

When the Old Testament was translated from Hebrew into Greek, the word *kyrios* was generally used to translate the sacred name of God. Of the 6,823 times that this name is used in the Hebrew, the Greek word *kyrios* ("Lord") is used to translate it on 6,156 occasions. This Greek word thus came to be an accepted way of referring directly and specifically to the God who had revealed himself to Israel at Sinai, and who had entered into a covenant with his people on that occasion. Jews would not use this term to refer to anyone or anything else. To do so would be to imply that this person or thing was of divine status. The historian Josephus tells us that the Jews refused to call the Roman Emperor *kyrios*, because they regarded this name as reserved for God alone.

Yet the writers of the New Testament had no hesitation in using this sacred name to refer to Jesus, with all that this implied. A name which was used exclusively to refer to God was regarded as referring equally to Jesus. This was not some error made by ill-informed writers, ignorant of the Jewish background to the name. After all, the first disciples were Jews. Those New Testament writers, such as Paul, who make most use of the term "Lord" to refer to Jesus were perfectly well aware of its implications. Yet they regarded the evidence concerning Jesus, especially his resurrection from the dead, as compelling them to make this statement concerning his identity. It was a deliberate, considered, informed, and justified decision, which is entirely appropriate in the light of the history of Jesus. He has been raised to glory and majesty, and sits at the right hand of God. He therefore shares the same status as God and is to be addressed accordingly.

Son of God

A further title used by the New Testament to refer to Jesus is "Son of God." In the Old Testament, the term is occasionally used to refer to angelic or supernatural persons (see Psalm 8:6; Job 38:7; Daniel 3:25). Messianic texts in the Old Testament refer to the coming Messiah as the "Son of God" (2 Samuel 7:12–14; Psalms 2:7; 86:26–7). The New Testament use of the term seems to mark a development of its Old Testament meaning, with an increased emphasis upon its exclusiveness.

Although all people are children of God in some sense of the word, the New Testament holds that Jesus is *the* Son of God. Paul distinguishes between Jesus as the natural Son of God, and believers as adopted sons. Their relation to God is quite different from Jesus' relationship to him, even though both may be referred to as "sons of God." We shall explore this point further when we consider the idea of adoption as a way of thinking about the benefits which Christ obtained for us on the cross. Similarly, in the First Letter of John, Jesus is referred to as "the Son," while believers are designated as "children." There is something quite distinct about Jesus' relation to God, as expressed in the title "Son of God."

The New Testament understanding of Jesus' relationship to God, expressed in the Father–Son relationship, takes a number of forms. First, we note that Jesus directly addresses God as "Father," using the Aramaic word "Abba," often thought to reflect a particularly close relationship (Mark 14:36; see also Matthew 6:9; 11:25–6; 26:42; Luke 23:34, 46). Secondly, it is clear from a number of passages that the evangelists regard Jesus as the Son of God, or that Jesus treats God as his father, even if this is not stated explicitly (Mark 1:11; 9:7; 12:6; 13:32; 14:61–2; 15:39). Thirdly, John's gospel is permeated with the Father–Son relationship (note especially passages such as John 5:16–27; 17:1–26), with a remarkable emphasis upon the identity of will and purpose of the Father and Son, indicating how close the relationship between Jesus and God was understood to be by the first Christians. At every level in the New Testament – in the words of Jesus himself, or in the impression which was created among the first Christians – Jesus is clearly understood to have a unique and intimate relationship to God, which the resurrection demonstrated publicly (Romans 1:3–4).

Son of Man

For many Christians, the term "Son of Man" stands as a natural counterpart to "Son of God." It is an affirmation of the humanity of Christ, just as the latter term is a complementary affirmation of his divinity. However, it is not quite as simple as this. The term "Son of Man" (Hebrew *ben adam* or Aramaic *bar nasha*) is used in three main contexts in the Old Testament:

1   As a form of address to the prophet Ezekiel.
2   To refer to a future eschatological figure (Daniel 7:13–14), whose coming signals the end of history and the start of divine judgment.
3   To emphasize the contrast between the lowliness and frailty of human nature and the elevated status or permanence of God and the angels (Numbers 23:19; Psalm 8:14).

The third such meaning relates naturally to the humanity of Jesus, and may underlie at least some of its references in the gospels of Matthew, Mark, and Luke. It is, however, the second use of the term which has attracted most scholarly attention.

The German New Testament scholar Rudolf Bultmann argued that Daniel 7:13–14 pointed to the expectation of the coming of a "Son of Man" at the end of history, and argued that Jesus shared this expectation. References by Jesus to "the Son of Man coming in clouds with great power and glory" (Mark 13:26) are thus, according to Bultmann, to be understood to refer to a figure *other than Jesus*. Bultmann suggested that the early church subsequently merged "Jesus" and "Son of Man," understanding them to be the one and the same. The early church thus invented the application of the term to Jesus.

This view has not, however, commanded universal assent. Other scholars have argued that the term "Son of Man" carries a range of associations, including suffering, vindication, and judgment, thus making it natural and proper to apply it to Jesus. George Caird is one New Testament scholar to develop such an approach, arguing that Jesus used the term "to indicate his essential unity with mankind, and above all with the weak and humble, and also his special function as predestined representative of the new Israel and bearer of God's judgment and kingdom."

God

Finally, we need to consider a group of New Testament texts which make the most important and exciting assertion of all: that Jesus is none other than God. All the other material we have considered in this chapter can be seen as pointing to this conclusion. The affirmation that Jesus is divine is the climax of the New Testament witness to the person of Jesus Christ. At least ten texts in the New Testament seem to speak explicitly of Jesus in this way (including John 1:1; 1:18; 20:28; Romans 9:5; Titus 2:13; Hebrews 1:8–9; 2 Peter 1:1; 1 John 5:20). Others point in this direction, implying much the same conclusion (such as Matthew 1:23; John 17:3; Galatians 2:20; Ephesians 5:5; Colossians 2:2; 2 Thessalonians 1:12; 1 Timothy 3:16).

We could continue this examination of the various titles which the New Testament employs to refer to Jesus, to illustrate the many facets of its complex witness to his identity and significance. There is, however, a danger that by doing this, we may miss seeing the wood for the trees. In other words, we will fail to see that these titles, together with the New Testament accounts of the impact Christ had upon those whom he encountered, build up to give a pattern. It is clear that the New Testament witnesses to Jesus as the embodiment of all God's promises, witnessed to in the Old Testament, brought to fulfillment and fruition.

The statements made about Jesus may be broadly listed under two classes. First, we have statements about Jesus' *function* – what God has done for us in Jesus. Second, we have statements about Jesus' *identity* – who Jesus is. The two are, of course, closely connected. His achievements are grounded in his identity; his identity is demonstrated in his achievements. As the pieces of a jigsaw puzzle build up to give a pattern, which no single piece can show on its own, so the New Testament "Christological titles" build up to give an overall picture, which no single title can adequately disclose. Taken collectively, they build up into a rich, deep, and powerfully persuasive portrait of Christ as the divine Savior and Lord, who continues to exercise an enormous influence over, and appeal to, sinful and mortal human beings.

Functional Statements About Jesus

Alongside statements concerning the *identity* of Jesus, there are several important New Testament passages which speak of the significance of Jesus in *functional* terms – that is to say, in terms which identify him as performing certain functions or tasks associated with God. Three groups of texts are of particular importance, as they identify the function of Jesus in terms which have clear implications for his identity.

Jesus is the savior of humanity

The Old Testament affirmed that there was only one savior of humanity: God. In the full knowledge that it was God alone who was Savior, that it was God alone who could save, the first Christians nevertheless affirmed that Jesus was Savior. As Athanasius (ca. 296–373) emphasized, no creature, no matter how great, can achieve this. If Jesus Christ has brought salvation to humanity, as the Creed declares that he has, then he must be God. If Jesus Christ is something other than God – in other words, a creature – then whatever "salvation" he brings is not the same as that offered by God.

A fish came to be a symbol of faith to the early Christians, as the five Greek letters spelling out "fish" in Greek (I-CH-TH-U-S) came to represent the slogan "Jesus Christ, Son of God, Savior." For the New Testament, Jesus saves his people from their sins (Matthew 1:21); in his name alone is there salvation (Acts 4:12); he is the "captain of salvation" (Hebrews 2:10); he is the "Savior, who is Christ the Lord" (Luke 2:11). And in these affirmations, and others, Jesus is understood to function as God, doing something which, properly speaking, only God can do.

Jesus is worshipped

Within the Jewish context in which the first Christians operated, it was God and God alone who was to be worshipped. Paul warned the Christians at Rome that there was a constant danger that humans would worship creatures, when they ought to be worshipping their creator (Romans 1:23). Yet the early Christian church worshipped Christ as God – a practice which is clearly reflected even in the New Testament. Thus, 1 Corinthians 1:2 speaks of Christians as those who "call upon the name of our Lord Jesus Christ," using language which reflects the Old Testament formulas for worshipping or adoring God (such as Genesis 4:26; 13:4; Psalm 105:1; Jeremiah 10:25; Joel 2:32). Jesus is thus clearly understood to function as God, in that he is an object of worship.

Jesus reveals God

"Anyone who has seen me, has seen the Father" (John 14:9). These remarkable words, so characteristic of John's gospel, emphasize the belief that the Father speaks and acts in the Son – in other words, that God is revealed in and by Jesus. To have seen Jesus is to have seen the Father – in other words, Jesus is understood, once more, to function as God.

These three groups of passages clearly point to an understanding of Jesus which transcends the category of pure humanity. Yet neither the New Testament writers, nor Christian theology, understand this to entail that Jesus is *not* a human being. For every biblical passage that explicitly affirms that Jesus was rather more than a human being, others can be brought forward that affirm that he was indeed a real human being. Jesus wept, suffered, became tired, and experienced human emotions.

One of the perennial tasks of Christian theology has been the clarification of the relationship between human and divine elements in the person of Jesus Christ. First, Jesus was a genuine human being. He was someone who felt pain, who knew what it was like to be hungry and thirsty. Yet this insight, on its own, is not enough to do justice to the biblical portrait of Jesus. We must turn to the second conclusion to understand why.

In the second place, the New Testament insists that Jesus was far more than a human being. Without in any way denying the real humanity of Jesus, the New Testament declares him to be the "Son of God," "Lord," and so forth. It applies words to him which are reserved for God, and attributes actions to him which are the privilege of God alone.

The Chalcedonian Definition

The riddle that Christian theology is called to resolve is how these two elements can be held together. A number of simple solutions were explored, only to be rejected, in the first period of Christian theological reflection. We may briefly note three of these inadequate approaches.

Adoptionism maintains that Jesus was basically a human being who was anointed by the Holy Spirit in the same way as the prophets of the Old Testament, but in a superior way. At his baptism by John the Baptist, Jesus was thus "adopted" by the Father and became God's Son. He was given a mission to preach the good news of the Kingdom, and empowered to work miracles. According to this view, Jesus belongs to the same lineage as all the prophets of the Old Testament – he was different in degree but not in kind.

Docetism (deriving from the Greek verb *dokein*, "to appear") argued that Jesus Christ was completely divine, but *appeared* also to be human. Although really divine, Christ presented himself to humanity as one who shared their condition.

Arianism (which takes its name from Arius, an Alexandrian writer of the fourth century) held that Jesus Christ was not divine, but was supreme among God's creatures.

The Council of Chalcedon (451) may be regarded as laying down a controlling principle for classical Christology, which has been accepted as definitive within much Christian theology. The principle in question could be summarized like this: provided that it is recognized that Jesus Christ is both truly divine and truly human, the precise manner in which this is articulated or explored is not of fundamental importance. Oxford patristic scholar Maurice Wiles summarized Chalcedon's aims as follows:

> On the one hand was the conviction that a savior must be fully divine; on the other was the conviction that what is not assumed is not healed. Or, to put the matter in other words, the source of salvation must be God; the locus of salvation must be humanity. It is quite clear that these two principles often pulled in opposite directions. The Council of Chalcedon was the church's attempt to resolve, or perhaps rather to agree to live with, that tension. Indeed, to accept both principles as strongly as did the early church is already to accept the Chalcedonian faith.

In part, Chalcedon's decision to insist upon the two natures of Christ, while accepting a plurality of interpretations regarding their relation, reflects the political situation of the period. At a time in which there was considerable disagreement within the church over the most reliable way of stating the "two natures of Christ," the council was obliged to adopt a realistic approach, and give its weight to whatever consensus it could find. That consensus concerned the recognition that Christ was both divine and human, but *not* how the divine and human natures related to each other.

The Christian doctrine of the person of Jesus Christ is often discussed in terms of "incarnation." "Incarnation" is a difficult yet important word, deriving from the Latin term for "flesh," summarizing and affirming the basic Christian belief that Jesus Christ is both divine and human. The idea of the Incarnation is the climax of Christian reflection upon the mystery of Christ – the recognition that Jesus Christ reveals God; that he represents God; that he speaks as God and for God; that he acts as God and for God; that he is God. In short, we must, in the words of a first-century writer, learn to "think about Jesus as we do about God" (2 Clement 1.1–2). We are thus in a position to take the crucial step which underlies all Christian thinking on the Incarnation – to say that, as Jesus Christ acts as God and for God in every context of importance, we should conclude that, for all intents and purposes, he is God.

Christ as Mediator

So how are we to conceive the identity of Christ? What models or analogies may be helpful as we try to visualize the place of Jesus Christ on the map of divine and human possibilities? In this section, we shall explore one New Testament title for Christ which is relatively easy to grasp, and consider its implications. The New Testament refers to Christ as a *mediator* between God and humanity at several points (e.g., Hebrews 9:15; 1 Timothy 2:5). Christ is here understood to mediate between a transcendent God and fallen humanity.

So what is mediated? Two basic complementary answers are given within the New Testament, and the long tradition of Christian theological engagement with scripture: *revelation* and *salvation*. Christ mediates both *knowledge of God* and *fellowship with God*.

The so-called "*Logos*-Christology" of Justin Martyr and other early patristic writers is an excellent instance of the notion of the mediation of knowledge of God through Christ. The *Logos* is understood to be a mediating principle which bridges the gap between a transcendent God and God's creation. Although present in a transient manner in the Old Testament prophets, the *Logos* becomes incarnate in Christ, and thus provides a point of mediation between God and humanity. A related approach is found in Emil Brunner's *The Mediator* (1927), and in a more developed form in his 1938 work *Truth as Encounter*. In the latter, Brunner argued that faith was primarily an encounter with the God who meets us personally in Jesus Christ.

Other writers have stressed the importance of Christ as the one who mediates salvation. This approach can be seen in John Calvin's *Institutes* (1559). Christ is here seen as a unique channel or focus, through which God's redeeming work is directed toward and made available to humanity. Humanity, as originally created by God, was good in every respect. On account of the Fall, natural human gifts and faculties have been radically impaired. As a consequence, both the human reason and human will are contaminated by sin. Unbelief is thus seen as an act of will as much as of reason; it is not simply a failure to discern the hand of God within the created order, but a deliberate decision *not* to discern it and *not* to obey God.

Calvin develops the consequences of this at two distinct, although clearly related, levels. At the revelational level, humans lack the necessary rational and volitional resources to discern God fully within the created order. There are obvious parallels here with the *Logos*-Christology of Justin Martyr. At the soteriological level, humans lack what is required in order to be saved; they do not *want* to be saved (on account of the debilitation of the mind and will through sin), and they are *incapable* of saving themselves (in that salvation presupposes obedience to God, now impossible on account of sin). True knowledge of God and salvation must both therefore come from outside the human situation. In such a manner, Calvin lays the foundations for his doctrine of the mediatorship of Jesus Christ.

Calvin's analysis of the knowledge of God and of human sin lays the foundation for his Christology. Jesus Christ is the mediator between God and humanity. In order to act as such a mediator, Jesus Christ must be both divine and human. In that it was impossible for us to ascend to God, on account of our sin, God chose to descend to us instead. Unless Jesus Christ was himself a human being, other human beings could not benefit from his presence or activity. "The Son of God became the Son of Man, and received what is ours in such a way that he transferred to us what is his, making that which is his by nature to become ours through grace."

Calvin's stress upon the mediatorial presence of God in Christ leads him to insist upon a close connection between the person and the work of Christ. Drawing on a tradition going back to Eusebius of Caesarea (ca. 260–ca. 340), Calvin argues that Christ's work may be summarized under three offices or ministries (the *munus triplex Christi*): prophet, priest, and king. The basic argument is that Jesus Christ brings together in his person the three great mediatorial offices of the Old Testament. In his *prophetic* office, Christ is the herald and witness of God's grace. He is a teacher endowed with divine wisdom and authority. In his *kingly* office, Christ has inaugurated a kingship which is heavenly, not earthly; spiritual, not physical. This kingship is exercised over believers through the action of the Holy Spirit. Finally, through his *priestly* office, Christ is able to reinstate us within the divine favor, through offering his death as a satisfaction for our sin. In all these respects, Christ brings to fulfillment the mediatorial ministries of the Old Covenant, allowing them to be seen in a new and clearer light as they find their fulfillment in his mediatorship.

Engaging with a Text

Dorothy L. Sayers is perhaps best known for her crime novels, which introduced Lord Peter Wimsey as an amateur aristocratic sleuth. However, she also developed a considerable interest in Christian theology, as the lecture below makes clear. The lecture was given during World War II, so the reference to totalitarianism would have resonated strongly with her audience. The basic theme is that it is not good enough to agree that Jesus had some useful ideas, unless we have good reasons for asserting that there is something distinctive about Jesus which requires us to take those ideas with compelling seriousness. Hence, Sayers argues, the great questions of Christology are inevitable, and must be addressed.

Sayers offered an important and penetrating analysis of the relation of the divinity and humanity of Christ in a lecture delivered in England in 1940, later published in a collection entitled *Creed or Chaos?* (1947). Using the rise of Nazism in Germany under Adolf Hitler during the 1930s as an example, she argues that claims to moral or cultural authority must be grounded in something intrinsic to the person of Christ. Otherwise, Christ will be judged by moral and cultural principles, instead of acting as their foundation and criterion.

If "the average man" is required to "believe in Christ" and accept His authority for "Christian principles," it is surely relevant to inquire who or what Christ is, and why His authority should be accepted. But the question, "What think ye of Christ?" lands the average man at once in the very knottiest kind of dogmatic riddle. It is quite useless to say that it doesn't matter particularly who or what Christ was or by what authority He did those things, and that even if He was only a man, He was a very nice man and we ought to live by His principles: for that is merely Humanism, and if the "average man" in Germany chooses to think that Hitler is a nicer sort of man with still more attractive principles, the Christian Humanist has no answer to make.

It is not true at all that dogma is "hopelessly irrelevant" to the life and thought of the average man. What is true is that ministers of the Christian religion often assert that it is, present it for consideration as though it were, and, in fact, by their faulty exposition of it make it so. The central dogma of the Incarnation is that by which relevance stands or falls. If Christ was only man, then He is entirely irrelevant to any thought about God; if He is only God, then He is entirely irrelevant to any experience of human life. It is, in the strictest sense, necessary to the salvation of relevance that a man should believe rightly the Incarnation of Our Lord Jesus Christ. Unless he believes rightly, there is not the faintest reason why he should believe at all. And in that case, it is wholly irrelevant to chatter about "Christian principles." . . . If the "average man" is going to be interested in Christ at all, it is the dogma that will provide the interest. The trouble is that, in nine cases out of ten, he has never been offered the dogma. What he has been offered is a set of technical theological terms which nobody has taken the trouble to translate into language relevant to ordinary life . . . Teachers and preachers never, I think, make it sufficiently clear that dogmas are not a set of arbitrary regulations invented *a priori* by a committee of theologians enjoying a bout of all-in dialectical wrestling. Most of them were hammered out under pressure of urgent practical necessity to provide an answer to heresy.

You may find the following questions helpful in interacting with this text, either on your own or in a group discussion.

1 Read through the opening paragraph. What point does Sayers make here? What is her fundamental criticism of "Christian Humanism"? How does she understand the question of the *identity* of Christ to shape our thinking on his relevance to life?

2 "If Christ was only man, then He is entirely irrelevant to any thought about God; if He is only God, then He is entirely irrelevant to any experience of human life." Locate this statement within the text. How does Sayers arrive at this conclusion? And how does she further develop the ideas contained in it?

3 Read through the concluding section of the extract. Some argue that doctrines about Jesus – for example, that he is both divine and human – just make a simple gospel un- necessarily complicated. What do you think Sayers might say in response to such objections?

CHAPTER 5

Salvation ✓

A central theme of the Christian message is that the human situation has, in some way, been transformed by the death and resurrection of Jesus Christ. In turning to explore the theology of salvation, we need to engage with two questions. First, there is the question of how "salvation" itself is to be understood. Second, there is the question of how salvation is possible, and in particular how it relates to the history of Jesus Christ. Both these questions have been the subject of intense discussion throughout Christian history, and we shall briefly consider some themes to emerge from this debate in what follows.

We begin by considering the first of these questions: what *is* salvation? One way of beginning a discussion of this issue is to look at some images of salvation used in Paul's letters.

Pauline Images of Salvation

Throughout his letters, Paul uses a rich range of images to illuminate and clarify what benefits Christ secures for believers. One such term is *salvation*. For understandable reasons, this term has often been seen as of primary importance, overshadowing the others. In fact, the term has a series of specific associations, which need to be appreciated. The basic notion is that of release from danger or captivity, including the idea of being delivered from some form of fatal illness. Notions such as "healing" and "liberation" can be seen as part of this important Pauline term. Paul sees salvation as having past (e.g., Romans 8:24), present (e.g., 1 Corinthians 1:18), and future (e.g., Romans 13:11) dimensions. It is a process that has been begun, but has yet to reach its fulfillment.

A second image of importance is that of *adoption*. At several points, Paul speaks of Christians as having been "adopted" into the family of God (Romans 8:15, 23; Galatians 4:5). It is widely thought that Paul is here drawing on a legal practice, common in Greco-Roman culture (yet, interestingly, not recognized within traditional Jewish law). According to many interpreters of Paul, to speak of "believers" having been adopted into the family of God is to make the point that believers share the same inheritance rights as Jesus Christ, and will hence receive the glory which Christ achieved (although only after first sharing in his sufferings).

At the time of the Reformation in the sixteenth century, many came to place particular importance on the image of *justification*. Especially in those letters dealing with the relation of Christianity to Judaism (such as Galatians and Romans), Paul affirms that believers have been "justified through faith" (e.g., Romans 5:1–2). This is widely held to involve a change in a believer's legal status in the sight of God, and their ultimate assurance of acquittal before God, despite their sinfulness. The term "justification" and the verb "to justify" thus came to signify "entering into a right relationship with God," or perhaps "being made righteous in the sight of God."

A fourth image is that of *redemption*. The main sense of this term is to "secure someone's release through payment." In the ancient world, which acted as the backdrop to Paul's thought, the term could be used to refer to the liberation of prisoners of war, or to the securing of liberty of those who had sold themselves into slavery, often to pay off a family debt. Paul's basic idea appears to be that the death of Christ secures the freedom of believers from slavery to the law or to death, in order that they might become slaves of God instead (1 Corinthians 6:20; 7:23).

The Problem of Analogy: Salvation as Ransom

In an earlier chapter, we noted how the theological use of analogies raised some interesting questions. How far can these analogies be pressed? For example, in thinking of God as "father," are we implying that God is male? A similar issue arises in connection with thinking about salvation, and we shall explore the question by looking at the image of salvation as a "ransom."

The image of Christ's death as a ransom came to be of central importance to Greek patristic writers, such as Irenaeus. The New Testament speaks of Jesus giving his life as a ransom for sinners (Mark 10:45; 1 Timothy 2:6). So what are the implications of this image? The word "ransom" suggests three related ideas:

1 *Liberation:* A ransom is something which achieves freedom for a person who is held in captivity.
2 *Payment:* A ransom is a sum of money which is paid in order to achieve someone's liberation.
3 *Someone to whom the ransom is paid:* A ransom is usually paid to a person's captor.

There is no doubt that the New Testament proclaims that we have been liberated from captivity through the death and resurrection of Jesus. We have been set free from captivity to sin and the fear of death (Romans 8:21; Hebrews 2:15). It is also clear that the New Testament understands the death of Jesus as the price which had to be paid to achieve our liberation (1 Corinthians 6:20; 7:23). In both these respects, the scriptural use of "redemption" corresponds to the everyday use of the word. But what of the third aspect?

The New Testament nowhere suggests that Jesus' death was the price paid to someone (such as the devil) to achieve our liberation. Some patristic writers, however, assumed that they could press this analogy to its limits, and declared that God had delivered us from the power of the devil by offering him Jesus as the price of our liberation.

Origen, perhaps the most speculative of early patristic theologians, was one such writer. If Christ's death was a ransom, Origen argued, it must have been paid to someone. But to whom? It could not have been paid to God, as God was not holding sinners to ransom. Therefore, it had to be paid to the devil.

Gregory the Great developed this idea still further. The devil had acquired rights over fallen humanity, which God was obliged to respect. The only means by which humanity could be released from this satanic domination and oppression was through the devil exceeding the limits of his authority, and thus being obliged to forfeit his rights. So how could this be achieved? Gregory suggests that it could come about if a sinless person were to enter the world, yet in the form of a normal sinful person. The devil would not notice until it was too late. In claiming authority over this sinless person, the devil would have overstepped the limits of his authority, and thus be obliged to forfeit his rights.

Gregory suggests the image of a baited hook, with Christ's humanity being the bait, and his divinity the hook. The devil, like a great sea-monster, snaps at the bait – and then discovers, too late, the hook. "The bait tempts in order that the hook may wound. Our Lord therefore, when coming for the redemption of humanity, made a kind of hook of himself for the death of the devil." Other writers explored other images for the same idea – that of trapping the devil. Christ's death was like a net for catching birds, or a trap for catching mice. It was this aspect of this approach to the meaning of the cross that caused the most disquiet subsequently. It seemed that God was guilty of deception.

This theme is probably best seen in the writings of Rufinus of Aquileia, particularly his exposition of the Apostles' Creed, which dates from around the year 400:

> [The purpose of the Incarnation] was that the divine virtue of the
> Son of God might be like a kind of hook hidden beneath the form
> of human flesh . . . to lure on the prince of this world to a
> contest; that the Son might offer him his human flesh as a bait
> and that the divinity which lay underneath might catch him and
> hold him fast with its hook . . . Then, just as a fish when it seizes a
> baited hook not only fails to drag off the bait but is itself dragged
> out of the water to serve as food for others; so he that had the
> power of death seized the body of Jesus in death, unaware of the
> hook of divinity which lay hidden inside. Having swallowed it, he
> was immediately caught. The gates of hell were broken, and he
> was, as it were, drawn up from the pit, to become food for others.

The imagery of victory over the devil proved to have enormous
popular appeal. The medieval idea of "the harrowing of hell"
bears witness to its power. According to this, after dying upon the
cross, Christ descended to hell, and broke down its gates in order
that the imprisoned souls might go free. The idea rested (rather
tenuously, it has to be said) upon 1 Peter 3:18–22, which makes
reference to Christ "preaching to the spirits in prison." The
hymn "Ye Choirs of New Jerusalem," written by Fulbert of
Chartres, expresses this theme in two of its verses, picking up
the theme of Christ as the "lion of Judah" (Revelation 5:5)
defeating Satan the serpent (Genesis 3:15):

> For Judah's lion bursts his chains
> Crushing the serpent's head;
> And cries aloud through death's domain
> To wake the imprisoned dead.
>   Devouring depths of hell their prey
> At his command restore;
> His ransomed hosts pursue their way
> Where Jesus goes before.

A similar idea is found in *Piers the Plowman*, one of the most
important English-language poems of the fourteenth century. In
this poem, Piers falls asleep, and dreams of Christ throwing open
the gates of hell, and speaking the following words to Satan:

Here is my soul as a ransom for all these sinful souls, to redeem those that are worthy. They are mine; they came from me, and therefore I have the better claim on them . . . You, by falsehood and crime and against all justice, took away what was mine, in my own domain; I, in fairness, recover them by paying the ransom, and by no other means. What you got by guile is won back by grace . . . And as a tree caused Adam and all mankind to die, so my gallows-tree shall bring them back to life.

Theories of Atonement

Having examined some biblical imagery for salvation, and how it is to be interpreted, we may now turn to consider how these themes have been explored and developed within the Christian theological tradition. This area of Christian theology is tradition-ally described as "theories of the atonement." The word "atone-ment" can be traced back to 1526, when the English writer William Tyndale was confronted with the task of translating the New Testament into English. There was, at that time, no English word which meant "reconciliation." Tyndale thus had to invent such a word: "at-one-ment." This word soon came to bear the meaning "the benefits which Jesus Christ brings to believers through his death upon the cross." This unfamiliar word is rarely used in modern English, and has a distinctively archaic flavor to it. Rather than convey the impression that Christian thought is totally out of date, theologians now generally prefer to speak of this area as "the doctrine of the work of Christ."

In what follows, we shall look at three approaches to the cross which have played a significant role in Christian theology. They by no means exhaust Christian reflection on this important theme.

The Cross as Sacrifice

The New Testament, drawing on Old Testament imagery and expectations, presents Christ's death upon the cross as a sacrifice.

This approach, which is especially associated with the Letter to the Hebrews, presents Christ's sacrificial offering as an effective and perfect sacrifice, which was able to accomplish that which the sacrifices of the Old Testament were only able to intimate, rather than achieve. In particular, Paul's use of the Greek term *hilasterion* (Romans 3:25) points to a sacrificial interpretation of Christ's death.

This idea is developed subsequently within the Christian tradition. In order for humanity to be restored to God, the mediator must sacrifice himself; without this sacrifice, such restoration is an impossibility. Athanasius argues that Christ's sacrifice was superior to those required under the Old Covenant in several respects:

> Christ offers a sacrifice which is trustworthy, of permanent effect, and which is unfailing in its nature. The sacrifices which were offered according to the Law were not trustworthy, since they had to be offered every day, and were again in need of purification. In contrast, the Savior's sacrifice was offered once only, and was accomplished in its entirety, and can thus be relied upon permanently.

This point is developed further in Athanasius' *Festal Letters*, written annually to celebrate the feast of Easter. In these letters, Athanasius develops the New Testament idea that there is an important analogy between the death of Christ on the cross and the sacrifice of a lamb during the Jewish festival of the Passover, commemorating Israel's deliverance from Egypt:

> [Christ], being truly of God the Father, became incarnate for our sakes, so that he might offer himself to the Father in our place, and redeem us through his offering and sacrifice . . . This is he who, in former times, was sacrificed as a lamb, having been foreshadowed in that lamb. But afterwards, he was slain for us. "For Christ, our passover, is sacrificed" (1 Corinthians 5:7).

Augustine of Hippo brought new clarity to the whole discussion of the nature of Christ's sacrifice through his crisp and highly influential definition of a sacrifice, set out in *City of God*:

"A true sacrifice is offered in every action which is designed to unite us to God in a holy fellowship." On the basis of this definition, Augustine has no difficulties in speaking of Christ's death as a sacrifice: "By his death, which is indeed the one and most true sacrifice offered for us, he purged, abolished, and extinguished whatever guilt there was by which the principalities and powers lawfully detained us to pay the penalty." In this sacrifice, Christ was both victim and priest; he offered himself up as a sacrifice: "He offered sacrifice for our sins. And where did he find that offering, the pure victim that he would offer? He offered himself, in that he could find no other."

This understanding of the sacrifice of Christ would become of decisive importance throughout the Middle Ages, and would shape Western understandings of Christ's death. In view of Augustine's importance, we may cite in full the passage which is often singled out as the most succinct expression of his thoughts on this matter:

> Thus the true Mediator, who "took the form of a servant" and was thus made "the mediator between God and humanity, the person Christ Jesus" (1 Timothy 2:5), receives the sacrifice in the "form of God" (Philippians 2:7, 8), in union with the Father, with whom he is one God. And yet, in the "form of a servant," he determined to be himself that sacrifice, rather than to receive it, in order to prevent anyone from thinking that such a sacrifice should be offered to any creature. Thus he is both the priest, who made the offering himself, and the oblation.

Hugh of St. Victor, writing in the early twelfth century, found the imagery of "sacrifice" helpful in explaining the inner logic of the workings of Christ's death on the cross. Christ was able to be an effective sacrifice for human sin precisely because he was able to bring our fallen sinful nature before God:

> From our nature, he took a victim for our nature, so that the whole burnt offering which was offered up might come from that which is ours. He did this so that the redemption to be offered might have a connection with us, through its being taken from

what is ours. We are truly made to be partakers in this redemption
if we are united through faith to the redeemer who has entered
into fellowship with us through his flesh.

The efficacy of Christ's sacrifice thus rested on his humanity, as
well as his divinity.

The Cross as a Victory

A second way of approaching the meaning of the cross integrates
a series of biblical passages focusing upon the notion of a divine
victory over hostile forces. The New Testament declares that God
has given us a victory through the resurrection of Jesus Christ.
"Thanks be to God, who gives us the victory through our Lord
Jesus Christ" (1 Corinthians 15:57). The early church gloried in
the triumph of Christ upon the cross, and the victory that he won
over sin, death, and Satan. But in what way may this victory be
understood? Who is it who has been defeated? And how? Christian writers of the first five centuries were deeply attracted by the
imagery of Christ gaining a victory through the cross. It was clear
to them that Christ had defeated death, sin, and the devil. Just as
David killed Goliath with his own weapons, so Christ defeated sin
with its weapon – death. Through an apparent defeat, victory was
gained over a host of hidden forces which tyrannized humanity.

Patristic writers such as Athanasius and Augustine of Hippo
used a number of central images to explore the nature of human
captivity to sin, and the manner in which we have been liberated
by Christ's death and resurrection. We were held in bondage by
the fear of death. We were imprisoned by sin. We were trapped by
the power of the devil. With great skill, these writers built up a
coherent picture of the human dilemma. Human beings are held
prisoner by hostile forces, and are unable to break free unaided.
Someone was required who would break into their prison, and
set them free. Someone from outside the human situation would
have to enter into our predicament, and liberate us. Someone
would have to cut the bonds which held us captive. Time and

time again, the same theme is restated: we are trapped in our situation, and our only hope lies in liberation from outside.

According to this approach, through his death and resurrection, Christ has confronted and disarmed the host of hostile forces which collectively held us in captivity. The cross and resurrection represent a dramatic act of divine liberation, in which God delivers his people from captivity to hostile powers, as he once delivered his people Israel from bondage in Egypt. The second-century writer Irenaeus of Lyons put it like this: "The Word of God was made flesh in order that he might destroy death and bring us to life. For we were tied and bound in sin, we were born in sin, and we live under the dominion of death."

This note of triumph led Christians to draw on an image from Roman culture of the late classical period in their depictions of the benefits won by Christ on the cross. The victory of Christ was depicted as a great triumphant procession, comparable to those of ancient Rome, in which the great military achievements of its heroes were celebrated. In its classical form, the triumphal parade accompanied the victorious hero from the Campus Martius through the streets of Rome, finally ending up at the temple of Jupiter on the Capitoline Hill. The parade was led by the general's soldiers, often carrying placards with slogans describing the general and his achievements, or showing maps of the territories he conquered. Other soldiers led carts containing booty that would be turned over to Rome's treasury. A section of the parade included prisoners, often the leaders of the defeated cities or countries, bound in chains.

It was a small step for Christian writers to transform this imagery into the proclamation of Christ as the conquering hero. This powerful symbolism was firmly grounded in the New Testament, which spoke of the victorious Christ as "making captivity a captive" (Ephesians 4:8). While this theme can be seen in some Christian art of this early period, its most dramatic impact was upon the hymns of the time. One of the greatest hymns of the Christian church, dating from this period, portrays Christ's triumphant procession and celebrates his defeat of his foes.

Venantius Honorius Clementianus Fortunatus (ca. 530–ca. 610) was born in Ceneda, near Treviso, in Northern Italy. He became a Christian at an early age, and studied at Ravenna and Milan. He gained a reputation for excellence in poetry and rhetoric, and went on to become bishop of Poitiers around 599. He is chiefly remembered for his poem *Vexilla regis prodeunt* – "the royal banners go forth." According to a well-established tradition, in the year 569, St. Radegunde presented a large fragment of what was believed to be the true cross of Christ to the town of Poitiers, in Southern Gaul. Radegunde had obtained this fragment from the Emperor Justin II. Fortunatus was the one chosen to receive the relic on its arrival at Poitiers. When the bearers of the holy fragment were some two miles distant from the town, Fortunatus, with a great gathering of believers and enthusiasts – some of whom were carrying banners, crosses, and other sacred emblems – went forth to meet them. As they marched, they sang this hymn, which Fortunatus had composed for the occasion. This was soon incorporated within the Passiontide office of the Western church, and is still widely used today in marking Holy Week within Western Christianity. The English translation is taken from the *Mediaeval Hymns and Sequences* (1851) of the great Victorian hymnologist and medievalist John Mason Neale (1818–66):

> The royal banners forward go,
> The cross shines forth in mystic glow;
> Where he in flesh, our flesh Who made,
> Our sentence bore, our ransom paid.
>
> O tree of glory, tree most fair,
> Ordained those holy limbs to bear,
> How bright in purple robe it stood,
> The purple of a Saviour's blood!
>
> Upon its arms, like balance true,
> He weighed the price for sinners due,
> The price which none but He could pay,
> And spoiled the spoiler of his prey.

Incidentally, we need to note the importance of Christian hymns and songs as means of making doctrinal statements. The hymnbooks of the Christian church are often its most important and most memorable statements of doctrine.

The Cross and Forgiveness

A third approach to the meaning of the death of Christ integrates a series of biblical passages dealing with notions of judgment and forgiveness. The understanding of the work of Christ outlined above has enormous attractions, not least on account of its highly dramatic character. It also, however, has some serious weaknesses. For the eleventh-century writer Anselm of Canterbury, two weaknesses were of particular importance. In the first place, it failed to explain why God should wish to redeem us. In the second place, it was of little value in understanding how Jesus Christ was involved in the process of redemption. Anselm felt that more explanation was required.

To meet this need, he developed an approach to the work of Christ which centers upon the rectitude of the created order. God created the world in a certain way, which expresses the divine nature. God also created human beings in order that they might have fellowship in eternity with their creator. This purpose, however, would seem to have been frustrated by human sin, which comes as a barrier between humanity and God. A fundamental disruption has thus been introduced into creation. Its moral ordering has been violated. The redemption of humanity is thus called for, in order that the natural rectitude of the created order may be restored. In this sense, Anselm understands redemption as a restoration of humanity to its original status within creation.

How, then, can we be redeemed? Anselm stresses that God is obliged to redeem us in a way that is consistent with the moral ordering of the creation, reflecting God's own nature. God cannot create the universe in one way, as an expression of God's will and nature, and then violate its moral order by acting in a completely different way in the redemption of humanity. God must redeem us in a way that is consistent with God's own nature and purposes. Redemption must, in the first place, be moral, and in the second place, be *seen* to be moral. God cannot employ one standard of morality at one point, and another later on. God is therefore under a self-imposed obligation to respect the moral order of the creation.

Having established this point, Anselm then considers how redemption is possible. The basic dilemma can be summarized as follows. God cannot restore us to fellowship with him, without first dealing with human sin. Sin is a disruption of the moral ordering of the universe. It represents the rebellion of the creation against its creator. It represents an insult and an offence to God. The situation must therefore be made right before fellowship between God and humanity can be restored. God must therefore "make good" the situation in a way that is consistent with both the divine mercy and the divine righteousness. Anselm thus introduces the concept of a "satisfaction" – a payment or other action which compensates for the offence of human sin. Once this satisfaction has been made, the situation can revert to normal. But this satisfaction must first be made.

The problem, Anselm observes, is that human beings do not have the ability to make this satisfaction. It lies beyond their resources. They need to make it – but they cannot. Humanity ought to make satisfaction for its sins, but cannot. God is under no obligation to make satisfaction – but God could do this, if it was appropriate. Therefore, Anselm argues, if God were to become a human being, the resulting God-person would have both the *obligation* (as a human being) and the *ability* (as God) to make the necessary satisfaction. Thus, the Incarnation leads to a just solution to the human dilemma. The death of Jesus Christ upon the cross demonstrates God's total opposition to sin, while at the same time providing the means by which sin could be really and truly forgiven, and the way opened to renewed fellowship between humanity and God.

The basic idea is that the value of the satisfaction thus offered had to be equivalent to the weight of human sin. Anselm argued that the Son of God became incarnate in order that Christ, as God incarnate, would possess both the human *obligation* to pay the satisfaction, and the divine *ability* to pay a satisfaction of the

magnitude necessary for redemption. This idea is faithfully repro-
duced by Mrs. Cecil F. Alexander in her famous nineteenth-
century hymn *There is a Green Hill Far Away*:

> There was no other good enough
> To pay the price of sin;
> He only could unlock the gate,
> Of heaven, and let us in.

The theological basis of the notion of "satisfaction" was developed further in the thirteenth century by Thomas Aquinas.
Aquinas grounds the adequacy of the "satisfaction of Christ" to
compensate for human sin in three considerations:

> A proper satisfaction comes about when someone offers to the
> person offended something which gives him a delight greater
> than his hatred of the offence. Now Christ by suffering as a result
> of love and obedience offered to God something greater than what
> might be exacted in compensation for the whole offence of human-
> ity; firstly, because of the greatness of the love, as a result of which
> he suffered; secondly, because of the worth of the life which he laid
> down for a satisfaction, which was the life of God and of a human
> being; thirdly, because of the comprehensiveness of his passion and
> the greatness of the sorrow which he took upon himself.

Aquinas here follows Anselm in arguing that the inherent worth
of Christ's death is grounded in his divinity. Why is Christ's death
so significant, and possessed of a capacity to redeem us? Because,
Aquinas argues, he – and he alone – is God incarnate. As Aquinas
puts it, "the worth of Christ's flesh is to be reckoned, not just
according to the nature of flesh but according to the person who
assumed it, in that it was the flesh of God, from whom it gained an
infinite worth." In response to the question of why the death of
one person should have possessed such saving significance, Aquinas points out that Christ's significance in this matter does not rest
on his humanity, but on his divinity.

Nevertheless, despite this emphasis on the divinity of Christ, it
is clear that Aquinas has taken care to ensure that the importance

of the humanity of Christ should not be overlooked. The first and third of his three considerations can each be argued to give a significant place to Christ's humanity in the process of redemption, by stressing the saving importance of Christ's love and suffering. Anselm tended to treat Christ's humanity as little more than the means by which Christ was able to justly bear the penalty due for human sin; Aquinas is thus able to offer a more positive assessment of the soteriological role of the humanity of Christ.

But how does Christ's achievement upon the cross affect us? In what way do we share in the benefits of his death and resurrection? Anselm felt that this point did not require discussion, and so gave no guidance on the matter. Later writers, however, felt that it needed to be addressed. Three main ways of understanding how believers relate to Christ in this manner may be noted.

1 *Participation.* Through faith, believers participate in Jesus Christ. They are "in Christ," to use Paul's famous phrase. They are caught up in him, and share in his risen life. As a result of this, they share in all the benefits won by Christ, through his obedience upon the cross.

2 *Representation.* Christ is the covenant representative of humanity. Through faith, we come to stand within the covenant between God and humanity. All that Christ has won for us is available to us, on account of the covenant. Just as God entered into a covenant with Israel, so God has entered into a similar covenant with his church. Christ, by his obedience upon the cross, represents God's covenant people, winning benefits for them as their representative. By coming to faith, individuals come to stand within the covenant, and thus participate in all its benefits, won by Christ.

3 *Substitution.* Christ is here understood to be our substitute. We ought to have been crucified, on account of our sins; Christ is crucified in our place. God allows Christ to stand in our place, taking our guilt upon himself, in order that Christ's righteousness, won by obedience upon the cross, might become ours.

Engaging with a Text

Our text for further study is taken from a sermon preached by Augustine of Hippo, one of the Christian church's greatest theologians. Augustine had a reputation as a lucid and powerful preacher, and his sermons include detailed yet very accessible accounts of the major themes of Christian theology. Unsurprisingly, Augustine regularly preached on the meaning of the cross, and the means by which Christ's death and resurrection secured human salvation. The sermon is based on the opening section of the fifth chapter of the Book of Revelation, which allows Augustine to explore how Christ can be thought of as both a lion and a lamb the "lion of Judah" and the "lamb of God," who takes away the sin of the world.

> If Christ had not been put to death, death would not have died. The devil was conquered by his own trophy of victory. The devil jumped for joy, when he seduced the first man, and cast him down to death. By seducing the first man, he killed him; by killing the last man, he lost the first from his snare. The victory of our Lord Jesus Christ came when he rose again from the dead, and ascended into heaven. It was at this point that the text from the Book of Revelation, which you heard read today, was fulfilled: "The lion of the tribe of Judah has won the day" (Revelation 5:5). The one who was slain as a lamb is now called a lion – a lion on account of his courage, a lamb on account of his innocence; a lion, because he was unconquered: a lamb, because of his gentleness. By his death, the slain lamb has conquered the lion who "goes around seeking someone to devour" (1 Peter 5:8). The devil, on the other hand, is here called a lion for his savagery, rather than his bravery . . . The devil jumped for joy when Christ died; and by the very death of Christ the devil was overcome: he took, as it were, the bait in the mousetrap. He rejoiced at Christ's death, believing himself to be the commander of death. But that which caused his joy dangled the bait before him. The Lord's cross was the devil's mousetrap: the bait which caught him was the death of the Lord.

After you have read through this text, try answering these questions, either on your own or in your discussion group.

1   Refresh your memory about the three major approaches to the meaning of the cross that we considered earlier in this chapter. Which of them seems to be the "best fit" for Augustine's approach?

2   Can you summarize, in your own words, the basic argument that Augustine sets out? In what way does Christ's death on the cross deliver humanity from its entanglement with the power of the devil, according to Augustine?

3   What does Augustine mean when he writes: "The Lord's cross was the devil's mousetrap"? What impact do you think this would have had on his audience? What point do you think he was trying to make?

CHAPTER 6

Trinity

For many, the doctrine of the Trinity is one of the most baffling areas of Christian theology. How can God be thought of as "three persons"? There are many who suspect that this is simply an attempt by theologians to make their subject inaccessible to outsiders. Thomas Jefferson, third president of the United States of America, was severely critical of what he termed the "incomprehensible jargon of the Trinitarian arithmetic." Why on earth do we need to speak of God in this convoluted and puzzling way?

The best way of understanding the doctrine is to suggest that it is the inevitable and legitimate way of thinking about God which emerges from a sustained engagement with the biblical witness to the words and works of God. The doctrine of the Trinity can be regarded as the outcome of a process of sustained and critical reflection on the pattern of divine activity revealed in scripture, and continued in Christian experience. This is not to say that scripture contains a doctrine of the Trinity; rather, scripture bears witness to a God who demands to be understood in a trinitarian manner.

At first sight, there are only two biblical verses which are open to a trinitarian interpretation: Matthew 28:19 and 2 Corinthians 13:14. The first commands the disciples to baptize people "in the name of the Father, Son and Holy Spirit"; the second speaks of the Father, Son, and Spirit in the familiar words of "the grace." Both these verses have become deeply rooted in the Christian consciousness, the former on account of its baptismal associations, and the latter through the common use of the formula in Christian prayer and devotion. Yet these two verses, taken together or in isolation, can hardly be thought of as constituting a doctrine of the Trinity.

The ultimate grounds of the doctrine of the Trinity are not to be sought exclusively in these two verses. Rather, the foundations of the doctrine are to be found in the pattern of divine activity to which the New Testament bears witness. The Father is revealed in Christ through the Spirit. There is the closest of connections between the Father, Son, and Spirit in the New Testament writings. Time after time, New Testament passages link together these three elements as part of a greater whole. The totality of God's saving presence and power can only, it would seem, be expressed by involving all three elements (for example, see 1 Corinthians 12:4–6; 2 Corinthians 1:21–2; Galatians 4:6; Ephesians 2:20–2; 2 Thessalonians 2:13–14; Titus 3:4–6; 1 Peter 1:2).

The development of the doctrine of the Trinity is best seen as being directly related to the evolution of Christology. The more emphatic the church became that Christ was God, the more it came under pressure to clarify how Christ related to God. The development of the doctrine of the Trinity took place in three stages, and was essentially complete by the end of the fourth century.

Stage 1   Recognition of the full divinity of Jesus Christ.
Stage 2   Recognition of the full divinity of the Spirit.
Stage 3   Definitive formulation of the doctrine of the Trinity, embedding and clarifying these central insights, and determining their mutual relationship.

This sequential development of the doctrine of the Trinity is acknowledged by Gregory of Nazianzus (329–89), who pointed to a gradual progress in clarification and understanding of the mystery of God's revelation in the course of time. It was, he argued, impossible to deal with the question of the divinity of the Spirit until the issue of the divinity of Christ had been settled:

> The Old Testament preached the Father openly and the Son more obscurely. The New Testament revealed the Son, and hinted at the divinity of the Holy Spirit. Now the Spirit dwells in us, and is revealed more clearly to us. It was not proper to preach the Son openly, while the divinity of the Father had not yet been admitted. Nor was it proper to accept the Holy Spirit before [the divinity of] the Son had been acknowledged . . . Instead, by gradual advances and . . . partial ascents, we should move forward and increase in clarity, so that the light of the Trinity should shine.

In view of the importance of the recognition of the divinity of the Holy Spirit to the development of the doctrine of the Trinity, we shall consider this in more detail.

The Holy Spirit

"God is spirit" (John 4:24). But what does this tell us about God? The English language uses at least three words – "wind," "breath," and "spirit" – to translate a single Hebrew term, *ruach*. This important Hebrew word has a depth of meaning which it is virtually impossible to reproduce in English. *Ruach*, traditionally translated simply as "spirit," is associated with a range of meanings, each of which casts some light on the complex associations of the Christian notion of the Holy Spirit.

Spirit as wind

The Old Testament writers are careful not to identify God with the wind, and thus reduce God to the level of a natural force.

Nevertheless, a parallel is drawn between the power of the wind and the power of God. To speak of God as spirit is to call to mind the surging energy of the "Lord of Hosts," and remind Israel of the power and dynamism of the God who had called Israel out of Egypt. This image of the Spirit as redemptive power is perhaps stated in its most significant form in the account of the exodus from Egypt, in which a powerful wind divides the Red Sea (Exodus 14:21). Here, the idea of *ruach* conveys both the power and the redemptive purpose of God.

The image of the wind also allowed the variety of human experience of God to be accounted for, and visualized in a genuinely helpful manner. The Old Testament writers were conscious of experiencing the presence and activity of God in two quite distinct manners. Sometimes God was experienced as a judge, one who condemned Israel for its waywardness; yet at other times, God is experienced as one who refreshes the chosen people, like water in a dry land. The image of the wind conveyed both these ideas in a powerful manner.

It must be remembered that Israel bordered the Mediterranean Sea to the west, and the great deserts to the east. When the wind blew from the east, it was experienced as a mist of fine sand which scorched vegetation and parched the land. Travelers' accounts of these winds speak of their remarkable force and power. Even the light of the sun is obliterated by the sandstorm thrown up by the wind. This wind was seen by the biblical writers as a model for the way in which God demonstrated the finitude and transitoriness of the creation. "The grass withers and the flowers fall, when the breath of the Lord blows on them" (Isaiah 40:7). Just as the scorching east wind, like the Arabian sirocco, destroyed plants and grass, so God was understood to destroy human pride (see Psalm 103:15–18; Jeremiah 4:11). Just as a plant springs up, fresh and green, only to be withered before the blast of the hot desert wind, so human empires rise only to fall before the face of God.

At the time when the Old Testament prophet Isaiah was writing, Israel was held captive in Babylon. To many, it seemed that the great Babylonian empire was a permanent historical feature, which nothing could change. Yet the transitoriness of human achievements when the "breath of the Lord" blows upon them is asserted by the prophet, as he proclaims the pending destruction of that empire. God alone is permanent, and all else is in a state of flux and change.

The western winds, however, were totally different. In the winter, the west and southwest winds brought rain to the dry land as they blew in from the sea. In the summer, the western winds did not bring rain, but coolness. The intensity of the desert heat was mitigated through these gentle cooling breezes. And just as this wind brought refreshment, by moistening the dry ground in winter and cooling the heat of the day in summer, so God was understood to refresh human spiritual needs. In a series of powerful images, God is compared by the Old Testament writers to the rain brought by the western wind (Hosea 6:3), refreshing the land.

Spirit as breath

The idea of spirit is associated with life. When God created Adam, God breathed into him the breath of life, as a result of which he became a "living being" (Genesis 2:7). The basic difference between a living and a dead human being is that the former breathes and the latter does not. This led to the idea that life was dependent upon breath. God is the one who breathes the breath of life into empty shells and brings them to life. God brought Adam to life by breathing into him. The famous Old Testament vision of the valley of the dry bones (Ezekiel 37:1–14) also illustrates this point. Can these dry bones live? The bones only come to life when breath enters into them (Ezekiel 37:9–10).

The model of God as spirit, therefore, conveys the fundamental insight that God is the one who gives life, even the one who is able to bring the dead back to life. It is thus important to note that *ruach* is often linked with God's work of creation (e.g., Genesis 1:2; Job 26:12–13; 33:4; Psalm 104:27–31), even if the precise role of the Spirit is left unspecified. There is clearly an association between Spirit and the giving of life through creation.

Spirit as charism

The technical term "charism" refers to the "filling of an individual with the Spirit of God," by which the person in question is enabled to perform tasks which would otherwise be impossible. The gift of wisdom is often portrayed as a consequence of the endowment of the Spirit (Genesis 41:38–9; Exodus 28:3; 35:31; Deuteronomy 34:9). At times, the Old Testament attributes gifts of leadership or military prowess to the influence of the Spirit (Judges 14:6, 19; 15:14, 15). However, the most pervasive aspect of this feature of the Spirit relates to the question of prophecy.

The Old Testament does not offer much in the way of clarification concerning the manner in which the prophets were inspired, guided, or motivated by the Holy Spirit. Before the Israelites were exiled in Babylon, prophecy was often associated with ecstatic experiences of God, linked with wild behavior (1 Samuel 10:6; 19:24). Nevertheless, the activity of prophecy gradually became associated with the *message* rather than the *behavior* of the prophet. The prophet's credentials rest upon an endowment with the Spirit (Isaiah 61:1; Ezekiel 2:1–2; Micah 3:8; Zechariah 7:12), which authenticates the prophet's message – a message which is usually described as "the word [*dabhar*] of the Lord."

But is the Holy Spirit *divine?* Athanasius and Basil of Caesarea argued that this was the case, and made an appeal to the formula which had by then become universally accepted for baptism. Since the time of the New Testament (see Matthew 28:18–20), Christians were baptized in the name of "the Father, Son, and Holy Spirit." Athanasius argued that this had momentous implications for an understanding of the status of the person of the Holy Spirit. In his *Letter to Serapion*, Athanasius declared that the baptismal formula clearly pointed to the Spirit sharing the same divinity as the Father and the Son. This argument eventually prevailed.

However, patristic writers were hesitant to speak openly of the Spirit as God, in that this practice was not sanctioned by scripture

– a point discussed at some length by Basil of Caesarea in his treatise on the Holy Spirit (374–5). Even as late as 380, Gregory of Nazianzus conceded that many Orthodox Christian theologians were uncertain as to whether to treat the Holy Spirit "as an activity, as a creator, or as God."

This caution can be seen in the final statement of the doctrine of the Holy Spirit formulated by a council meeting at Constantinople in 381. The Spirit was here described, not as God, but as "the Lord and giver of life, who proceeds from the Father, and is worshipped and glorified with the Father and Son." The language is unequivocal: the Spirit is to be treated as having the same dignity and rank as the Father and Son, even if the term "God" is not to be used explicitly.

Three factors were of special importance in establishing the divinity of the Holy Spirit during the later fourth century. First, as Gregory of Nazianzus stressed, scripture applied all the titles of God to the Spirit, with the exception of "unbegotten." Gregory drew particular attention to the use of the word "holy" to refer to the Spirit, arguing that this holiness did not result from any external source, but was the direct consequence of the nature of the Spirit. The Spirit was to be considered as the one who sanctifies, rather than the one who requires to be sanctified.

Second, the functions which are specific to the Holy Spirit establish the divinity of the Spirit. Didymus the Blind (d. 398) was one of many writers to point out that the Spirit was responsible for the creating, renewing, and sanctification of God's creatures. Yet how could one creature renew or sanctify another creature? Only if the Spirit was divine could sense be made of these functions. If the Holy Spirit performed functions which were specific to God, it must follow that the Holy Spirit shares in the divine nature. This point is stated with particular clarity by Basil of Caesarea:

> All who are in need of sanctification turn to the Spirit; all those seek him who live by virtue, for his breath refreshes them and comes to their aid in the pursuit of their natural and proper end. Capable of perfecting others, the Spirit himself lacks nothing. He

is not a being who needs to restore his strength, but himself supplies life . . . Souls in which the Spirit dwells, illuminated by the Spirit, themselves become spiritual and send forth their grace to others. From here comes foreknowledge of the future, understanding of mysteries, apprehension of what is hidden, the sharing of the gifts of grace, heavenly citizenship, a place in the chorus of angels, joy without end, abiding in God, being made like God and – the greatest of them all – being made God.

For Basil, the Spirit makes creatures both to be like God and to be God – and only one who is divine can bring this about. (In chapter 4, we explored how this same argument was also used to infer the divinity of Christ from the fact that the New Testament recognized him as "savior.")

Third, the reference to the Spirit in the baptismal formula of the church was interpreted as supporting the divinity of the Spirit. Baptism took place in the name of the "Father, Son, and Holy Spirit" (Matthew 28:17–20). Athanasius and others argued that this formula established the closest of connections between the three members of the Trinity, making it impossible to suggest that the Father and Son shared in the substance of the Godhead, while the Spirit was nothing other than a creature. In a similar way, Basil of Caesarea argued that the baptismal formula clearly implied the inseparability of Father, Son, and Spirit. This verbal association, according to Basil, clearly had considerable theological implications.

With the full recognition of the divinity of the Holy Spirit in the fourth century, the scene was set for the final development of the Christian doctrine of the Trinity.

The Doctrine of the Trinity

The starting point for Christian reflections on the Trinity is, as we have seen, the New Testament witness to the presence and activity of God in Christ and through the Spirit. For Irenaeus, the whole process of salvation, from its beginning to its end, bore witness to the action of Father, Son, and Holy Spirit. Irenaeus made use of a phrase which would feature prominently in future discussions of the Trinity: "the economy of salvation." The term "economy" here needs a little explanation. The Greek word *oikonomia* basically means "the way in which one's affairs are ordered" (the relation to the modern sense of the word will thus be clear). For Irenaeus, "the economy of salvation" meant "the way in which God has ordered the salvation of humanity in history."

At the time, Irenaeus was under considerable pressure from Gnostic critics, who argued that the creator God was quite distinct from (and inferior to) the redeemer God (see chapter 3). Marcion argued that the Old Testament God was merely a creator God, and totally different from the redeemer God of the New Testament. As a result, the Old Testament should be shunned by Christians, who should concentrate their attention upon the New Testament. Irenaeus vigorously rejected this idea. He insisted that the entire process of salvation, from the first moment of creation to the last moment of history, was the work of the one and the same God. There was a single economy of salvation, in which the one God – who was both creator and redeemer – was at work to redeem the creation.

In his *Demonstration of the Apostolic Preaching*, Irenaeus insisted upon the distinct yet related roles of Father, Son, and Spirit within the economy of salvation. He affirmed his faith in

> *God the Father uncreated*, who is uncontained, invisible, one God, creator of the universe; this is the first article of our faith . . . And the *Word of God*, the Son of God, our Lord Jesus Christ, . . . who, in the fullness of time, in order to gather all things to himself, he became a human being amongst human beings, capable of being seen and touched, to destroy death, bring life, and restore fellowship between God and humanity. And the *Holy Spirit* . . . who, in the fullness of time, was poured out in a new way on our human nature in order to renew humanity throughout the entire world in the sight of God.

This passage brings out clearly the idea of the Godhead in which each person is responsible for an aspect of the economy of salvation. Far from being a rather pointless piece of theological speculation, the doctrine of the Trinity is grounded directly in the complex human experience of redemption in Christ, and is concerned with the explanation of this experience.

Tertullian argued that God's action within the economy of salvation is complex, revealing both a *unity* and a *distinctiveness*. The doctrine of the Trinity thus affirms the unity of God, while recognizing the complexity and profundity of the Christian vision of God. Tertullian thus argues that *substance* is what unites the three aspects of the economy of salvation; *person* is what distinguishes them. The three persons of the Trinity are distinct, yet not divided (*distincti non divisi*); different, yet not separate or independent of each other (*discreti non separati*). The complexity of the human experience of redemption is thus the result of the three persons of the Godhead acting in distinct yet coordinated manners in human history, without any loss of the total unity of the Godhead.

The real difficulty for most people lies in the *visualization* of the Trinity. How can we make sense of such a complex and abstract idea? St. Patrick, the patron saint of Ireland, is rumored to have used the leaf of a shamrock to illustrate how a single leaf could have three different elements. Gregory of Nyssa uses a series of analogies in his letters to help his readers grasp the reality of the Trinity, including:

1   The analogy of a spring, fount and stream of water. The one flows from the other and they share the same substance – water. Although different aspects of the stream of water may be *distinguished*, they cannot be *separated*.
2   The analogy of a chain. There are many links in a chain; yet to be connected to one is to be connected to all of them. In the same way, Gregory argues, someone who encounters the Holy Spirit also encounters the Father and the Son.
3   The analogy of a rainbow. Drawing on the Nicene statement that Christ is "light from light," Gregory argues that the rainbow allows us to distinguish and appreciate the different

colors of a sunbeam. There is only one beam of light, yet the colors blend seamlessly into one another.

In what follows, we shall explore one more recent way of thinking about the Trinity which has proved very helpful to many. It is associated with the contemporary American theologian Robert Jenson, and is set out in his work *The Triune Identity: God According to the Gospel* (1982).

The Trinity and the Naming of God

To understand Jenson's approach, we may ask a simple question: who is the God of Israel? One answer might be that God is God; as there is no other god, there is nothing further to discuss. But remember that ancient Israel existed in a polytheistic context. There were many "gods." It was a perfectly fair question to ask which one Israel regarded as its own. In other words, the God who Israel knew and worshipped needed to be identified – to be *named*. The Old Testament declares that the God of Israel is the god who revealed himself to Abraham, Isaac, and Jacob; the god who led the people of Israel out of Egypt and into the promised land with great signs and wonders. In other words, we name God by telling the story of God.

You might do the same sort of thing when trying to identify a person. Your conversation with someone might go like this: "You know John Brown? You don't. Well, do you remember reading about a man who managed to row a boat all the way across the Atlantic Ocean about a year ago? The boat nearly sank at one point. And when he finished the journey, he wrote a book about it? Ah! You *do* know who I mean!" What you are doing here is telling a story which centers on John Brown. You are identifying him in this way. John Brown is the person at the center of the story. And so it is with God and the Old Testament. The Old Testament identifies God from the history of God's people – the great stories of Abraham, Isaac, and Jacob, of the exodus from

Egypt, and so on, are told in order to identify God. The God of Israel is the one who acted in this way.

This is made clear in a number of Old Testament passages (e.g., Exodus 19:4–5; Deuteronomy 26:5–9; Ezekiel 20:5–26). Question: who is God? Answer: God is the one who delivered Israel from Egypt. Of course, God has a name as well – a name which proves difficult to translate into English, "Yahweh," "the Lord," and "Jehovah" being three of the best-known translations. But the fact remains that God is usually thought of in terms of God's actions.

Now we turn to the God who Christians worship and adore. Who is this God? To answer this question, the New Testament tells a story – perhaps the most famous story in the world – the story of Jesus Christ. And as that story reaches its climax in the account of the resurrection of Jesus from the dead, we learn that God, for Christians, is the one who acted in this way to raise Jesus. Question: who is the God who Christians worship and adore? Answer: whoever "raised Jesus our Lord from the dead" (Romans 4:24). Of course, the New Testament writers make it abundantly clear that the one who "raised Jesus our Lord from the dead" is the same God who delivered Israel from Egypt, thus affirming the continuity between the Old and New Testaments.

This idea can be taken further without difficulty. The resurrection of Jesus and the pouring out of the Spirit at Pentecost are treated as closely related by the New Testament. The complexity of the New Testament's statements concerning the relationship of God, Jesus, and the Spirit defies neat categorization. It is, however, clear that "God" is the one who raised Jesus from the dead, and is now present in the church through the Holy Spirit. In many ways, the Christian slogan "Father, Son, and Holy Spirit" (Matthew 28:19; 2 Corinthians 13:14) corresponds to the Old Testament slogan "the God of Abraham, Isaac, and Jacob" – it *identifies* the God in question. Question: what God are you talking about? Answer: the God who raised Jesus Christ from the dead, and is now present through the Spirit.

The trinitarian formula can thus be thought of as a *proper name* – a shorthand way of identifying exactly what God we are talking about. Christianity packs into this one neat phrase the high points of salvation history, the big moments (resurrection and Pentecost) when God was so clearly present and active. It specifically links God with these events, just as Israel specifically linked God with the exodus from Egypt. It focuses our attention on certain specific events, in which God's presence and activity were to be found concentrated and publicly demonstrated.

The doctrine of the Trinity can thus be seen as a summary of the story of God's dealings with Israel and the church. It narrates the story of how God created and redeemed humanity, affirming that it is the story of the one and the same God throughout. If you were talking about a great modern statesman, such as Winston Churchill or John F. Kennedy, you'd concentrate upon the high points of their careers – the moments when they stepped on to the stage of history, in order to change its direction. And the doctrine of the Trinity identifies those great moments in the history of salvation, when God was active and was seen to be active. It affirms that God is active in the world, that God is made known by God's actions, and points to the creation, the death and resurrection of Jesus Christ, and Pentecost as turning points in God's dealings with us. The doctrine of the Trinity thus spells out exactly who the God we are dealing with actually is.

Jenson develops this approach in a fresh and helpful direction, offering a creative restatement of the traditional doctrine of the Trinity. In *The Triune Identity* Jenson argues that "Father, Son, and Holy Spirit" is the proper name for the God whom Christians know in and through Jesus Christ. It is imperative, he argues, that God should have a proper name. "Trinitarian discourse is Christianity's effort to identify the God who has claimed us. The doctrine of the Trinity comprises both a proper name, "Father, Son and Holy Spirit" . . . and an elaborate development and analysis of corresponding identifying descriptions." Jenson points out that ancient Israel was set in a polytheistic context, in which the term "god" conveyed relatively little information. It was necessary to *name* the god in question. A similar situation was confronted by the writers of the New Testament, who were obliged to identify the god at the heart of their faith, and distinguish this god from the many other gods worshipped and acknowledged in the region, especially in Asia Minor.

The doctrine of the Trinity thus *identifies* and *names* the Christian God – but identifies and names this God in a manner consistent with the biblical witness. It is not a name which we have chosen; it is a name which has been chosen for us, and which we are authorized to use. In this way, Jenson defends the priority of God's self-revelation against human constructions of concepts of divinity. "The gospel identifies its God thus: God is the one who raised Israel's Jesus from the dead. The whole task of theology can be described as the unpacking of this sentence in various ways. One of these produces the church's trinitarian language and thought." The doctrine of the Trinity, Jenson affirms, allows the church to discover the distinctiveness of its creed, and avoid becoming absorbed by rival conceptions of God.

The doctrine of the Trinity thus centers on the recognition that God is named by scripture, and within the witness of the church. Within the Hebraic tradition, God is identified by historical events. Jenson notes how many Old Testament texts identify God with reference to divine acts in history – such as the liberation of Israel from its captivity in Egypt. The same pattern is evident in the New Testament: God is identified with reference to specific historical events, supremely the resurrection of Jesus Christ. God comes to be identified in relation to Jesus Christ. Who is God? Which god are we talking about? The God who raised Christ from the dead. As Jenson puts it, "the emergence of a semantic pattern in which the uses of 'God' and 'Jesus Christ' are mutually determining" is of fundamental importance within the New Testament.

> The gospel of the New Testament is the provision of a new identifying description for this same God [as that of Israel]. The coming-to-apply of this new description is the event, the witness to which is the whole point of the New Testament. God, in the gospel, is "whoever raised Jesus from the dead." Identification of God by the resurrection did not replace identification by the exodus; it is

essential to the God who raised Jesus that he is the same one who freed Israel. But the new thing that is the content of the gospel is that God has now identified himself also as "him that raised from the dead Jesus our Lord" (Romans 4:24). In the New Testament such phrases become the standard way of referring to God.

Jenson thus recovers a personal conception of God from metaphysical speculation. "Father, Son, and Holy Spirit" is a *proper name*, which we are asked to use in naming and addressing God. "Linguistic means of identification – proper names, identifying descriptions, or both – are a necessity of religion. Prayers, like other requests and praises, must be addressed." The Trinity is thus an instrument of theological precision, which forces us to be explicit about the God under discussion. Christians do not believe in a generic god, but in a very specific God who is known in and through a series of actions in history.

Engaging with a Text

Karl Barth is widely regarded as one of the greatest theologians of the twentieth century, and is widely credited with the rediscovery of interest in the doctrine of the Trinity in recent decades. Barth's ideas on the Trinity are difficult to grasp, and this section will therefore offer much more explanation than normal.

> The question of the self-revealing God which thus forces itself upon us as the first question cannot, if we follow the witness of scripture, be separated in any way from the second question: How does it come about, how is it actual, that this God reveals Himself? Nor can it be separated from the third question: What is the result? What does this event do to the man to whom it happens? Conversely, the second and third questions cannot possibly be separated from the first . . . *God* reveals Himself. He reveals Himself *through Himself.* He reveals *Himself.* If we really want to understand revelation in terms of its subject, i.e., God, then the first thing that we have to realize is that this subject, God, the revealer, is identical with His act in revelation, and also with its effect. It is from this fact, which in the first instance we are merely

indicating, that we learn we must begin the doctrine of revelation with the doctrine of the triune God.

"*God* reveals Himself. He reveals Himself *through Himself*. He reveals *Himself*." With these (decidedly non-inclusive, I fear) words, Barth sets up the revelational framework which leads to the formulation of the doctrine of the Trinity. *Deus dixit!* "God has spoken" in revelation, and it is the task of theology to inquire what this revelation presupposes and implies. For Barth, theology is a process of "thinking afterwards" about what is contained in God's self-revelation. We have to "inquire carefully into the relation between our knowing of God, and God himself in his being and nature."

With such statements, Barth sets up the context of the doctrine of the Trinity: given that God's self-revelation has taken place, what must be true of God if this can have happened? What does the actuality of revelation have to tell us about the being of God? Barth's starting point for his discussion of the Trinity is not a doctrine or an idea, but the actuality of God's speaking and God's being heard. For how can God be heard, when sinful humanity is incapable of hearing the Word of God?

The above is simply a paraphrase of sections of the first half-volume of Barth's *Church Dogmatics*, entitled "The Doctrine of the Word of God," punctuated by occasional quotations. There is an enormous amount being said in this, and it requires unpacking. Two themes need to be carefully noted:

1   Sinful humanity is fundamentally incapable of hearing the Word of God.
2   Nevertheless, sinful humanity has heard the Word of God, in that this Word makes its sinfulness known to it.

The very fact that revelation takes place thus requires explanation. For Barth, this implies that humanity is passive in the process of reception; the process of revelation is, from its beginning to its end, subject to the sovereignty of God as Lord. For revelation to *be* revelation, God must be capable of effecting self-revelation to sinful humanity, despite their sinfulness.

Once this paradox has been appreciated, the general structure of Barth's doctrine of the Trinity can be followed. In revelation, Barth argues, God must be as shown in the divine self-revelation. There must be a direct correspondence between the revealer and the revelation. If "God reveals himself as Lord" (a characteristically Barthian assertion), then God must be Lord "antecedently in himself." Revelation is the reiteration in time of what God actually is in eternity. There is thus a direct correspondence between:

1 the revealing God;
2 the self-revelation of God.

To put this in the language of trinitarian theology, the Father is revealed in the Son.

So what about the Spirit? Here we come to what is perhaps the most difficult aspect of Barth's doctrine of the Trinity: the idea of "revealedness" (*Offenbarsein*). To explore this, we will have to use an illustration not used by Barth himself. Imagine two individuals, walking outside Jerusalem on a spring day around the year AD 30. They see three men being crucified, and pause to watch. The first points to the central figure, and says: "There is a common criminal being executed." The second, pointing to the same man, replies: "There is the Son of God dying for me." To say that Jesus is the self-revelation of God will not do in itself; there must be some means by which Jesus is *recognized* as the self-revelation of God. It is this recognition of revelation as revelation that constitutes the idea of *Offenbarsein*.

How is this insight achieved? Barth is quite clear: sinful humanity is not capable of reaching this insight unaided. Barth is not prepared to allow humanity any positive role in the interpretation of revelation, believing that this is to subject divine revelation to human theories of knowledge. The recognition of revelation *as* revelation must itself be the work of God – more accurately, the work of the Spirit. Humanity does not become capable of hearing the word of the Lord (*capax verbi domini*), and then act in response to having heard that word; both the hearing and capacity to hear are given in the one act by the Spirit.

Barth's achievement was to demonstrate that the concepts of revelation and the Trinity were so completely interlocked and interwoven that neither could be affirmed without the other. To believe in a revealing God is implicitly to believe in a trinitarian conception of God, which it is the task of theology to unfold and explore. For Barth, the doctrine of the Trinity is thus presupposed by the entire project of Christian theology. While many would express reservations at aspects of his approach, few would deny that Barth's achievement represents a massive theological landmark.

CHAPTER 7

Church

The Apostle's Creed includes a clause which declares that Christians believe in the church. So what does this mean? How is the church to be defined, and what is its purpose? This area of theology is traditionally called "ecclesiology" (from *ekklesia*, the Greek word for "church"). It is one of the more delicate areas of theology, as it raises awkward denominational questions which are of central importance to the identity of churches. In this chapter, we shall explore a number of aspects of the doctrine of the church. As always, limits on space restrict the extent to which certain ideas can be discussed, and prevent us from looking at some issues which are of considerable interest.

The Church: Local or Universal?

The New Testament uses the word "church" in two somewhat different manners. At many points, the term "church" is used to designate individual Christian congregations – local, visible gatherings of believers. For example, Paul wrote letters to churches in the cities of Corinth and Philippi. The Book of Revelation makes reference to the "seven churches of Asia," probably meaning seven local Christian communities in the region of Asia Minor (modern-day Turkey). Yet, at other points, we find the term being used in a wider, more general sense, meaning something like "the total body of Christian believers." The tension between the local and universal senses of the word "church" is of considerable importance, and needs careful examination. How could both aspects be maintained?

Traditionally, this tension is resolved through arguing that there is one, universal church which exists in local communities. On the basis of this approach, there is one universal church, consisting of all Christian believers, which takes the form of individual local churches in a given region. One influential way of conceiving this distinction is due to John Calvin, who drew an important distinction between the *visible* and the *invisible* church. At one level, the church is the community of Christian believers, a visible group. It is also, however, the fellowship of saints and the company of the elect – an *invisible* entity. In its invisible aspect, the church is the invisible assembly of the elect, known only to God; in its visible aspect, it is the community of believers on earth. The former consists only of the elect; the latter includes both good and evil, elect and reprobate. The former is an object of faith and hope, the latter of present experience. The distinction between them is eschatological (that is, to do with the end times): the invisible church is the church which will come into being at the end of time, as God ushers in the final judgment of humanity.

Calvin's ideas were given more formal expression in the *Westminster Confession of Faith*, a document which has had considerable influence in Puritan and Reformed church circles:

> The catholic or universal church, which is invisible, consists of the whole number of the elect that have been, are, or shall be gathered into one, under Christ the head thereof . . . The visible church, which is also catholic or universal under the gospel (not confined to one nation as before under the law), consists of all those

throughout the world that profess the true religion, together with their children.

The importance of this model, and others like it, is best appreciated by considering the following question. How can we talk about "one" Christian church, when there are so many different Christian denominations?

Only One Church?

Faced with this apparent tension between a theoretical belief in "one church" and the brute observable reality of a plurality of churches, Christian writers developed approaches to allow the latter observation to be incorporated within the framework of the former. Four major approaches to the issue of the unity of the church may be noted, each of which possesses distinctive strengths and weaknesses.

1 An *imperialist* approach, which declares that there is only one empirical – that is, observable – church which deserves to be known and treated as the true church. All others are fraudulent pretenders to this title, or are at best little more than approximations to the real thing. This position was maintained by the Roman Catholic church prior to the Second Vatican Council (1962–5), which took the momentous step of recognizing other Christian churches as "separated" Christian brothers and sisters.

2 A *Platonic* approach, which draws a fundamental distinction between the empirical church (that is, the church as a visible historical reality) and the ideal church. This has found relatively little support in mainstream Christian theology, although some scholars have suggested that some such idea may lie behind Calvin's distinction between the "visible" and "invisible" church. However, as we noted above, this distinction is better interpreted along eschatological lines.

3   An *eschatological* approach, which suggests that the present disunity of the church will be abolished on the last day. The present situation is temporary, and will be resolved on the day of judgment. This understanding lies behind Calvin's distinction between the "visible" and "invisible" churches, which we considered above.

4   A *biological* approach, which likens the historical evolution of the church to the development of the branches of a tree. This image, developed by the eighteenth-century German Pietist writer Nicolas von Zinzendorf, and taken up with enthusiasm by Anglican writers of the following century, allows the different empirical churches – e.g., the Roman Catholic, Orthodox, and Anglican churches – to be seen as possessing an organic unity, despite their institutional differences.

In recent years, many theologians concerned with ecumenism (deriving from the Greek word *oecumene*, "the whole world," and now generally understood to mean "the movement concerned with the fostering of Christian unity") argued that the true basis of the "unity of the church" required to be recovered, after centuries of distortion. The maxim *ubi Christus, ibi ecclesia* ("where Christ is, there is also the church"), which derives from Ignatius of Antioch, pointed to the unity of the church lying in Christ, rather than in any historical or cultural factor. Throughout the New Testament, they argued, the diversity of local churches is not regarded as compromising the unity of the church. The church already possesses a unity through its common calling from God, which expresses itself in different communities in different cultures and situations. "Unity" must not be understood *sociologically* or *organizationally*, but *theologically*. Hans Küng stresses this point in his magisterial study *The Church*:

> The unity of the church is a spiritual entity. It is one and the same God who gathers the scattered from all places and all ages and makes them into one people of God. It is one and the same Christ who through his word and Spirit unites all together in the same

bond of fellowship of the same body of Christ . . . The Church *is* one, and therefore *should be* one.

The point that Küng makes is that the unity of the church is grounded in the saving work of God in Christ. This is in no way inconsistent with that one church adapting itself to local cultural conditions, leading to the formation of local churches. As Küng puts it:

> The unity of the church presupposes a multiplicity of churches; the various churches do not need to deny their origins or their specific situations; their language, their history, their customs and traditions, their way of life and thought, their personal structure will differ fundamentally, and no one has the right to take this from them. The same thing is not suitable for everyone, at every time, and in every place.

Discussion of the universality of the church has often focused on the idea of "catholicity," which needs more detailed explanation.

The Catholicity of the Church

In modern English, the term "catholic" is often confused, especially in non-religious circles, with "Roman Catholic." Although this confusion is understandable, it must be pointed out that it is not only Roman Catholics who are catholic, just as it is by no means only Eastern Orthodox writers who are orthodox in their theology. Indeed, many Protestant churches, more than a little embarrassed by the use of the term "catholic" in the creeds, have replaced it with the less contentious word "universal," arguing that this brings greater intelligibility to belief in "one holy universal and apostolic church."

The term "catholic" derives from the Greek phrase *kath' holou* ("referring to the whole"). The Greek words subsequently found their way into the Latin word *catholicus*, which came to have the meaning "universal or general." This sense of the word is retained in the English phrase "catholic taste," meaning a "wide-ranging taste" rather than a "taste for things that are Roman Catholic." Older versions of the English Bible often refer to some of the New Testament letters (such as those of James and John) as "catholic epistles," meaning that they are directed to all Christians (unlike those of Paul, which are directed to the needs and situations of individual identified churches, such as those at Rome or Corinth).

The developed sense of the word is perhaps best seen in the fourth-century catechetical writings of Cyril of Jerusalem. In his eighteenth catechetical lecture, Cyril teases out a number of senses of the word "catholic":

> The church is thus called "catholic" because it is spread throughout the entire inhabited world (*oikoumene*), from one end to the other, and because it teaches in its totality (*katholikos*) and without leaving anything out every doctrine which people need to know relating to things visible and invisible, whether in heaven and earth. It is also called "catholic" because it brings to obedience every sort of person – whether rulers or their subjects, the educated and the unlearned. It also makes available a universal (*katholikos*) remedy and cure to every kind of sin.

It will be clear that Cyril is using the term "catholic" in four ways, each of which deserves comment.

1 Catholic is to be understood as "spread throughout the entire inhabited world." Here, Cyril notes the geographical sense of the word. The notion of "wholeness" or "universality" is thus understood to mandate the church to spread into every region of the world.

2 Catholic means "without leaving anything out." With this phrase, Cyril stresses that the "catholicity" of the church involves the complete proclamation and explanation of the Christian faith. It is an invitation to ensure that the totality of the gospel is preached and taught.

3   Catholic means that the church extends its mission and min-
    istry to "every sort of person." Cyril here makes an essentially
    sociological point. The gospel and the church are for all kinds
    of human beings, irrespective of their race, gender, or social
    status. We can see here a clear echo of St. Paul's famous
    declaration that "there is neither Jew nor Greek, there is
    neither slave nor free, there is neither male nor female; for
    you are all one in Christ Jesus" (Galatians 3:28).
4   Catholic means that the church offers and proclaims "a uni-
    versal remedy and cure to every kind of sin." Here, Cyril
    makes a soteriological statement: the gospel, and the church
    which proclaims that gospel, can meet every human need and
    distress. Whatever sins there may be, the church is able to
    offer an antidote.

The various senses of the term "catholic" are also brought out
clearly by Thomas Aquinas, in his discussion of the section of the
Apostles' Creed dealing with the doctrine of the church. In this
analysis, Aquinas singles out three essential aspects of the idea of
"catholicity."

> The church is catholic, i.e., universal, first with respect to place,
> because it is throughout the entire world (*per totum mundum*),
> against the Donatists. See Romans 1:8: "Your faith is proclaimed
> in all the world"; Mark 16:15: "Go into all the world and preach
> the gospel to the whole creation."   Secondly, the church is
> universal with respect to the condition of people, because no one
> is rejected, whether master or slave, male or female. See Galatians
> 3:28: "There is neither male nor female." Thirdly, it is universal
> with respect to time. For some have said that the church should
> last until a certain time, but this is false, because this church began
> from the time of Abel and will last to the end of the world. See
> Matthew 28:20: "And I am with you always, to the close of the
> age." And after the close of the age it will remain in heaven.

Note how catholicity is here understood in terms of geographical, anthropological, and chronological universality.

The Church: Holy or Just Human?

One of the most interesting debates concerning the doctrine of the church is about whether its members are required to be holy. The debate is seen at its most intense during the Donatist controversy of the fourth century, which focused on the question of whether church leaders were required to be morally pure. Under the Roman Emperor Diocletian (284–313), the Christian church was subject to various degrees of persecution. The origins of the persecution date from 303; it finally ended with the conversion of Constantine, and the issuing of the Edict of Milan in 313. Under an edict of February 303, Christian books were ordered to be burned and churches demolished. Those Christian leaders who handed over their books to be burned came to be known as *traditores* – "those who handed over [their books]." The modern word "traitor" derives from the same root. One such *traditor* was Felix of Aptunga, who later consecrated Caecilian as bishop of the great North African city of Carthage in 311.

Many local Christians were outraged that such a person should have been allowed to be involved in this consecration, and declared that they could not accept the authority of Caecilian as a result. The new bishop's authority was compromised, it was argued, on account of the fact that the bishop who had consecrated him had lapsed under the pressure of persecution. The hierarchy of the Catholic church was thus tainted as a result of this development. The church ought to be pure, and should not be permitted to include such people. By the time Augustine (destined to be a central figure in the controversy) returned to North Africa from Rome in 388, a breakaway faction had established itself as the leading Christian body in the region, with especially strong support from the local African population.

The Donatists believed that the entire sacramental system of the Catholic church had become corrupted on account of the lapse of its leaders. How could the sacraments be validly administered by people who were tainted in this way? It was therefore necessary to replace these people with more acceptable leaders, who had remained firm in their faith under persecution. It was also necessary to rebaptize and reordain all those who had been baptized and ordained by those who had lapsed. Inevitably, this resulted in the formation of a breakaway faction. By the time Augustine returned to Africa, the breakaway faction was larger than the church from which it had originally broken away.

Augustine responded by putting forward a theory of the church which he believed was more firmly grounded in the New Testament than the Donatist teaching. In particular, Augustine emphasized the *sinfulness of Christians*. The church is not meant to be a "pure body," a society of saints, but a "mixed body" (*corpus permixtum*) of saints and sinners. Augustine finds this image in two biblical parables: the parable of the net which catches many fishes, and the parable of the wheat and the weeds (or "tares," to use an older word familiar to readers of the King James Bible). It is this latter parable (Matthew 13:24–31) which is of especial importance, and requires further discussion.

The parable tells of a farmer who sowed seed, and discovered that the resulting crop included both wheat and weeds. What could be done about it? To attempt to separate the wheat and the weeds while both were still growing would be to court disaster, probably involving damaging the wheat while trying to get rid of the weeds. But at the harvest, all the plants – whether wheat or weeds – are cut down and sorted out, thus avoiding damaging the wheat. The separation of the good and the evil thus takes place at the end of time, not in history.

For Augustine, this parable refers to the church in the world. It must expect to find itself including both saints and sinners. To attempt a separation in this world is premature and improper. That separation will take place in God's own time, at the end of history. No human can make that judgment or separation in God's place.

So in what sense is the church holy? For Augustine, the holiness in question is not that of its members, but of Christ. The church cannot be a congregation of saints in this world, in that its members are contaminated with original sin. However, the church is sanctified and made holy by Christ – a holiness which will be perfected and finally realized at the last judgment. In addition to this theological analysis, Augustine makes the practical observation that the Donatists failed to live up to their own high standards of morality. The Donatists, Augustine suggests, were just as capable as Catholics of getting drunk or beating people up.

Yet the Donatist vision of a "pure body" remains attractive to many. As is so often the case with theological debates, the evidence is never entirely on one side of the argument. A strong case continues to be made for the idea of the church as a "pure body," especially in denominations which trace their identity back to the more radical wing of the Protestant Reformation, often known as "Anabaptism." The radical Reformation conceived of the church as an "alternative society" within the mainstream of sixteenth-century European culture. For Menno Simmons, the church was "an assembly of the righteous," at odds with the world, and not a "mixed body," as Augustine argued:

> In truth, those who merely boast of his name are not the true congregation of Christ. The true congregation of Christ is those who are truly converted, who are born from above of God, who are of a regenerate mind by the operation of the Holy Spirit through the hearing of the Word of God, and have become the children of God.

It will be clear that there are strong parallels with the Donatist view of the church as a holy and pure body, isolated from the corrupting influences of the world, and prepared to maintain its purity and distinctiveness by whatever disciplinary means proved necessary.

Anabaptism maintained discipline within its communities through "the ban" – a means by which church members could be excluded from Anabaptist congregations. This means of discipline was regarded as essential to the identity of a true church. Part of the Anabaptist case for radical separation from the mainstream churches (a practice which continues to this day among the Amish of Lancaster County, Pennsylvania) was the failure of those churches to maintain proper discipline within their ranks.

The Schleitheim Confession grounded its doctrine of the "ban" on Christ's words, as they are recorded in Matthew 18:15–20:

> The ban shall be used in the case of all those who have given themselves to the Lord, to walk in his commandments, and with all those who are baptized into the one body of Christ and are called brothers or sisters, yet who lapse on occasion, and inadvertently fall into error and sin. Such people shall be admonished twice in secret, and on the third occasion, they shall be disciplined publicly, or banned according to the command of Christ (Matthew 18).

The "ban" was seen as being both deterrent and remedial in its effects, providing both an incentive for banned individuals to amend their way of life and a disincentive for others to imitate them in their sin. The Polish Racovian Catechism lists five reasons for maintaining rigorous discipline within Anabaptist communities, most of which reflect its policy of radical separation:

1 So that the fallen church member may be healed, and brought back into fellowship with the church.
2 To deter others from committing the same offense.
3 To eliminate scandal and disorder from the church.
4 To prevent the word of the Lord falling into disrepute outside the congregation.
5 To prevent the glory of the Lord being profaned.

Despite its pastoral intentions, the "ban" often came to be interpreted harshly, with congregation members often avoiding all social contact (known as "shunning") with both the banned individual and his or her family.

Other writers have pointed out how the term "holy" is often equated with "morality," "sanctity," or "purity," which often seem to bear little relation to the behavior of fallen human beings. Yet the Hebrew term *kadad*, which underlies the New Testament concept of "holiness," has a rather different meaning, bearing the sense of "being cut off," or "being separated." There are strong overtones of *dedication*: to be "holy" is to be set apart for and dedicated to the service of God.

A fundamental element – indeed, perhaps *the* fundamental element – of the Old Testament idea of holiness is that of "something or someone whom God has set apart." The New Testament restricts the idea almost entirely to personal holiness. It refers the idea to individuals, declining to pick up the idea of "holy places" or "holy things." People are "holy" in that they are dedicated to God, and distinguished from the world on account of their calling by God. A number of theologians have suggested a correlation between the idea of "the church" (the Greek word for which can bear the meaning of "those who are called out") and "holy" (that is, those who have been separated from the world, on account of their having been called by God).

To speak of the "holiness of the church" is thus primarily to speak of the holiness of the one who called that church and its members. The church has been separated from the world, in order to bear witness to the grace and salvation of God. In this sense, there are obvious connections between the church being "holy" and the church being "apostolic." The term "holy" is theological, not moral, in its connotations, affirming the calling of the church and its members, and the hope that the church will one day share in the life and glory of God.

So if the church is not defined by holiness, what is its distinguishing feature? A number of responses have been offered to this question, and we shall consider one of them in what follows.

The Church as Constituted by the Word

It will be clear from our discussion thus far that Christian theologians insist that the term "church" is to be defined theologically, not sociologically. To "believe in the church" is not to trust in the institution of the church, but to affirm that the church is ultimately called into being by God, with a mission and authorization which derive from God. A central theme of the Protestant understanding of the nature and mission of the church focuses on the presence of Christ resulting from the proclamation of his word, in preaching and the sacraments. For Martin Luther, the church is the community called into being by the preaching of God's word:

> Now, anywhere you hear or see [the Word of God] preached, believed, confessed, and acted upon, do not doubt that the true holy catholic church, a "holy Christian people" must be there, even though there are very few of them. For God's word "shall not return empty" (Isaiah 55:11), but must possess at least a fourth or a part of the field. And even if there were no other sign than this alone, it would be enough to prove that a holy Christian people must exist there, for God's word cannot be without God's people and conversely, God's people cannot be without God's word. For who would preach the word, or hear it preached, if there were no people of God? And what could or would God's people believe, If there were no word of God?

An episcopally ordained ministry is therefore not necessary to safeguard the existence of the church, whereas the preaching of the gospel is essential to the identity of that church. "Where the word is, there is faith; and where faith is, there is the true church." The visible church is constituted by the preaching of the word of God: no human assembly may claim to be the "church of God" unless it is founded on this gospel. It is more important to preach the same gospel as the apostles than to be a member of an institution which is historically derived from them

Calvin's teaching on the nature of the church takes a similar line, again stressing the importance of the proclamation of God's word as definitive of the identity of a church:

> Wherever we see the Word of God purely preached and listened to, and the sacraments administered according to Christ's institution, it is in no way to be doubted that a church of God exists. For his promise cannot fail: "Wherever two or three are gathered in my name, there I am in the midst of them" (Matthew 18:20) . . . If the ministry has the Word and honors it, if it has the administration of the sacraments, it deserves without doubt to be held and considered a church.

For Calvin, the preaching of the word and right administration of the sacraments are linked with the presence of Christ – and wherever Christ is, there his church is to be found as well.

This kerygmatic (from the Greek *kerygma*, meaning "herald") theme has continued to be of major importance in the twentieth century, particularly in the writings of Karl Barth. For Barth, the church is the community which comes into being in response to the proclamation of the word of God. The church is seen as a kerygmatic community which proclaims the good news of what God has done for humanity in Christ, and which comes into being wherever the word of God is faithfully proclaimed and accepted. As Barth put it in his 1948 address to the World Council of Churches, the church consists of "the gathering together (*congregatio*) of those men and women (*fidelium*) whom the living Lord Jesus Christ chooses and calls to be witnesses of the victory he has already won, and heralds of its future manifestation." Barth's ecclesiology is thoroughly trinitarian at this point, involving Father, Son, and Spirit in a dynamic understanding of the nature of the church. For Barth, the church is not an extension of Christ, but is united with Christ, and called and commissioned by him to serve the world. Christ is present within his church, through the Holy Spirit.

The role of the Holy Spirit is particularly important. Although it would not be correct to say that Barth has a "charismatic" understanding of the church, his Christological approach to the identity of the church allocates a definite and distinctive role to the Holy Spirit, which Barth summarized as follows in his *Dogmatics in Outline*:

> *Credo ecclesiam* ["I believe in the church"] means that I believe that here, at this place, in this assembly, the work of the Holy Spirit takes place. By that is not intended a deification of the creature; the church is not the object of faith, we do not believe *in* the church; but we do believe that in this congregation the work of the Holy Spirit becomes an event.

The church is thus seen as an event, not an institution. Barth does not identify the Holy Spirit with the church, nor limit the operation of the Spirit to the bounds of the institution of the church. He argues that the Spirit empowers and renews the church, unites it with Christ's redemptive work on the cross, and is the means by which the risen Christ is made present to the people of God. In this way, the Spirit safeguards the church from lapsing into purely secular ways of understanding its identity and mission.

For many Protestant theologians, the key concept of "apostolicity" means *conforming to the teaching of the apostles* – in other words, maintaining doctrinal continuity with the apostles through grounding belief and practice in scripture. Others, however, would place the emphasis elsewhere. Many Catholic theologians, for example, would argue that *institutional continuity* is essential to the identity of the church. More radical Protestant voices, especially within Anabaptism, argued that it was essential to include discipline in any definition of the church. How else could the purity and distinctiveness of the church be maintained?

Pure or Mixed Body: What Difference Does it Make?

Earlier in this chapter, we explored two rather different understandings of the observable or "empirical" church. One of these argues that the church is a "mixed body" of saints and sinners; the other that the church is (or ought to be) a pure body. So what difference does this make to ministry? How does theology impact on practice? We may note some points briefly.

A pure-body ecclesiology assumes that the members of the church are doctrinally and morally pure. It is therefore able to assume a very high level of commitment on their part. Evangelism is something that church members do outside the church. Preaching is primarily about deepening their knowledge of their faith, and encouraging them in their social and personal responsibilities as believers. For the same reason, such ecclesiologies often lead to an emphasis being placed on discipline. If a church is defined by doctrinal and moral purity, there must be means of enforcing this purity, otherwise the existence and integrity of the church is called into question. Earlier, we noted the "ban" as a means of securing this discipline; other approaches are, of course, possible.

A mixed-body ecclesiology must assume far less commitment on the part of its members. Evangelism is now something that must be done within the congregation itself. Preaching may take the form of encouraging congregational members in their social and personal responsibilities as believers; it must also, however, deal with the fact that some members will not be converted. Correspondingly, a lesser degree of commitment can be expected from the congregation as a whole, even though many individual members will be very committed to their faith. Since this ecclesiology does not demand moral or doctrinal purity on the part of its members, there is no need for means of enforcing this within the congregation. Most churches adopting this ecclesiology demand such purity from their ministers, but not from their members.

Engaging with a Text

One way of understanding the church is to see it as the sphere of God's transforming love for humanity. Some theologians argued that the church could be seen as a walled garden – rather like the original garden of Eden – in which believers could grow in grace and holiness, protected from the world around them. This approach to the Christian church develops the notion of a closed and protected community, within which faith, hope, and love may blossom, and individuals may live in tranquility with each other and with God. The church is called and fashioned out of the world in much the same way as a garden is an enclosed portion of wilderness, which can be watered, cultivated, and tended. The church is thus an Edenic community, seeking to recover the values of paradise within its own bounds. This idea is found in the writings of Ephrem the Syrian (d. 373), who regularly asserted that the church was not merely the gateway to paradise; in some way, a paradisiacal realm was established within its walls.

This idea is also found in a hymn by the great English writer Isaac Watts (1674–1748). Although Watts is probably best known for *When I survey the wondrous Cross*, he also penned a hymn which deals with the nature of the church:

> We are a garden walled around,
> Chosen and made peculiar ground;
> A little spot enclosed by grace
> Out of the world's wide wilderness.

> Like trees of myrrh and spice we stand,
> Planted by God the Father's hand;
> And all his springs in Zion flow,
> To make the young plantation grow.

> Awake, O, heavenly wind! and come,
> Blow on this garden of perfume;
> Spirit divine! descend and breathe
> A gracious gale on plants beneath.

The imagery derives from Augustine of Hippo, who pointed out that, in the Old Testament book of the Song of Songs, the church is described as "an enclosed garden, my sister and bride, a sealed fountain, a well of living water, an orchard of choice fruit" (Song of Songs 1:12 13). Watts develops this imagery. You may find the following questions helpful in interacting with his text.

1 In the first verse, Watts uses the phrase "peculiar ground." What do you think he means by this? At this time, the English word "peculiar" bore the meaning of "special." In what way does Watts' text help identify what is distinctive about the church?

2 Note the use of wilderness imagery in this verse. This was popular at the time: John Bunyan's famous work *Pilgrim's*

Progress refers to a journey through the "wilderness of the world." What do you think Watts hopes to demonstrate by contrasting the garden of the church with the wilderness of the world? How does this imagery help us understand his views on the nature and ministry of the church?

3   How do you think that the image of a garden helps Watts unfold the idea that the church is a place of spiritual growth and development? Does he see this process as something that we achieve, or something that is enabled and guided by God? What is the significance of his reference to the "heavenly wind" in the final verse?

CHAPTER 8

Heaven

Most works of Christian theology follow the pattern of the creeds, and end with a discussion of eternal life. This traditional approach will also be followed in this basic introduction to the themes of Christian theology. The term "eschatology" (from the Greek words *ta eschata*, meaning "last things") is widely used in Christian theology to refer to beliefs about judgment, heaven, and so forth. In this final chapter, we shall explore some aspects of Christian thinking about heaven.

Christianity is a religion of hope, which focuses on the resurrection of Jesus as the grounds for believing and trusting in a God who is able to triumph over death, and give hope to all those who suffer and die. The word "eschatology" is used to refer to Christian teachings about the "last things." Just as "Christology" refers to the Christian understanding of the nature and identity of Jesus Christ, so "eschatology" refers to the Christian understanding of such things as heaven and eternal life.

The eschatology of the New Testament is complex. However, one of its leading themes is that something which happened in the past has inaugurated something new, which will reach its final consummation in the future. The Christian believer is thus caught up in this tension between the "now" and the "not yet." In one sense, heaven has not yet happened; in another, its powerful lure already impacts upon us in a dramatic and complex fashion, in which we are at one and the same time excited at its prospect and dejected through knowing that we are not yet there.

The term "heaven" is used frequently in the Pauline writings of the New Testament to refer to the Christian hope. Although it is natural to think of heaven as a future entity, Paul's thinking appears to include both a future reality and a spiritual sphere or realm which coexists with the material world of space and time. Thus "heaven" is referred to both as the future home of the believer (2 Corinthians 5:1–2; Philippians 3:20) and as the present dwelling place of Jesus Christ, from which he will come in final judgment (Romans 10:6; 1 Thessalonians 1:10; 4:16).

As we shall see, one of Paul's most significant statements concerning heaven is the notion of believers being "citizens of heaven" (Philippians 3:20), and in some way sharing in the life of heaven in the present. The tension between the "now" and the "not yet" is evident in Paul's statements concerning heaven, making it very difficult to sustain the simple idea of heaven as something which will not come into being until the future, or which cannot be experienced at all in the present. For Paul, the hope of heaven impacts upon life in the here and now, even though heaven, in all its fullness, remains to be consummated in the future.

One helpful way of thinking about the modest New Testament statements on this subject is to see heaven as a consummation of the Christian doctrine of salvation. This states that the presence, penalty, and power of sin have all been finally eliminated, and the total presence of God in individuals and the community of faith has been achieved. Some such idea underlies the vision of heaven set out in the *Catechism of the Catholic Church*:

> Heaven is the ultimate end and fulfillment of the deepest human longings, the state of supreme, definitive happiness . . . this consummation will be the final realization of the unity of the human

race, which God willed from creation and of which the pilgrim Church has been "in the nature of sacrament." Those who are united with Christ will form the community of the redeemed, "the holy city" of God, "the Bride, the wife of the Lamb." She will not be wounded any longer by sin, stains, self-love, that destroy or wound the earthly community. The beatific vision, in which God opens himself in an inexhaustible way to the elect, will be the ever-flowing well-spring of happiness, peace, and mutual communion.

The New Testament parables of heaven are strongly communal in nature. Heaven is here portrayed as a banquet, a wedding feast, or as a city – the New Jerusalem. Eternal life is thus not a projection of an individual human existence, but is rather to be seen as sharing, with the redeemed community as a whole, in the community of a loving God.

We begin our exploration of the theology of heaven by examining a biblical image which is of central importance to our theme.

An Image of Heaven: The New Jerusalem

We have already seen how Christian theologians struggled to do intellectual justice to immensely difficult ideas, such as the "two natures" of Jesus Christ, or the doctrine of the Trinity. Yet theologians are also called to explore images – such as God as a shepherd, or a father. As the Oxford scholar and theologian Austin Farrer argued, Christianity represents a "rebirth of images." Great importance was assigned to images in conceiving and sustaining the Christian life. New impetus was also given to the religious imagery which the church inherited from Israel. In the case of the Christian understanding of heaven, it is an image, rather than an idea, which plays a decisively important role for Christian theology – namely, the image of the "New Jerusalem."

Many Old Testament passages speak of the city of Jerusalem, which is seen both as a tangible image of the presence and providence of God within its sturdy walls, and also as a pointer to the fulfillment of Messianic expectations. Jerusalem was the city within which the great Israelite king David established his throne and built a temple to the "Lord God of Israel." As a result, there was a strong expectation that this was the city within which the coming Messiah would dwell. The New Testament gives this a new twist, not least in the remarkable reworking of the theme of the "city of God" found in the Book of Revelation, the final book of the Christian Bible. For this biblical writer, the fulfillment of all Christian hopes and expectations centers upon the New Jerusalem, the city of God within which the risen Christ reigns triumphant. This image has stimulated intense reflection on the part of Christian theologians. The image of the New Jerusalem has exercised a decisively important influence over Christian reflection on heaven down the centuries.

The powerful imagery in the Book of Revelation has saturated Christian hymns and theology, particularly the church's ideas on how heaven is to be visualized. The consolation of heaven is here contrasted with the suffering, tragedy, and pain of life on earth. Traditionally, the Book of Revelation – also known as the Apocalypse – is believed to reflect the social exclusion and perhaps persecution faced by Christians in a region of the Roman empire in the later years of the reign of the Emperor Domitian. Perhaps its most enduring image – and certainly that most relevant to this study – is its portrayal of the New Jerusalem:

> Then I saw a new heaven and a new earth; for the first heaven and the first earth had passed away, and the sea was no more. And I saw the holy city, the new Jerusalem, coming down out of heaven from God, prepared as a bride adorned for her husband. And I heard a loud voice from the throne saying, "See, the home of God is among mortals. He will dwell with them; they will be his peoples, and God himself will be with them; he will wipe every tear from their eyes. Death will be no more; mourning and crying and pain will be no more, for the first things have passed away." And the one who was seated on the throne said, "See, I am making all things new." (Revelation 21:1–5)

In this passage, the theme of the New Jerusalem is integrated with motifs drawn from the creation account – such as the presence of the "tree of life" (Revelation 22:2) – suggesting that heaven can be seen as the restoration of the bliss of the garden of Eden (Genesis 2), when God dwelt with humanity in harmony. The pain, sorrow, and evil of a fallen world have finally passed away, and the creation is restored to its original intention. The Christians of Asia Minor at this time were few in number, and generally of low social status. There is no doubt that they derived much consolation from the anticipation of entering a heavenly city which vastly exceeded any earthly comforts or security they had known. The holy city was paved with gold and decked with jewels and precious stones, dazzling its inhabitants and intensifying the longing to enter through its gates on the part of those still on earth.

The New Jerusalem – like its earthly counterpart – is portrayed as a walled city. Its security is beyond question. It is perched on the peak of a hill that no invading army could hope to ascend. Its walls are so thick that they could not be breached by any known siege engine, and so high that no human could hope to scale them. Its twelve gates are guarded by angels. Just as a return to Eden was once prevented by a guardian angel, so the New Jerusalem is defended against invasion by supernatural forces.

It is important to note that the twelve gates of the New Jerusalem, though guarded by angels, are permanently thrown open. Whereas the classic fortified city of ancient times was designed to exclude outsiders, the architecture of the New Jerusalem seems designed to welcome them within its boundaries. The city is portrayed as perfectly cubical (21.36), perhaps signifying that it is a perfection of the square temple which the prophet Ezekiel envisaged for the rebuilt Jerusalem after the Israelites' return from exile (Ezekiel 43:16; 48:20).

The careful attention paid to imagery suggests that the New Jerusalem should be seen in terms of the fulfillment of Israel through the restoration of its twelve tribes (Revelation 21:12–14). Most significantly of all, the New Jerusalem does not contain a temple (21:22). The cultic hierarchies of the old priestly tradition are swept to one side. Everyone is now a priest, and there is no need for a temple because God dwells within the city as a whole. Indeed, in a remarkable reworking of these images, the city has itself become a temple, in that God is now to be found at every place within it, rather than being located only within one specific building. The Old Testament prophets had yearned for the rebuilding of the temple, but now Revelation declares that it has become redundant. What that rebuilding foreshadowed has now taken place. With the advent of the reality of God's presence, the symbol of the temple was no longer required. The dwelling place of God is now with the people of God; it can no longer be contained within a physical structure. The New Jerusalem is thus characterized by the pervasive presence of God, and the triumphant and joyful response of those who had long awaited this experience.

This image of heaven resonates strongly with one of the leading themes of Paul's theology – that Christians are to be regarded as "citizens of heaven" (Philippians 3:19–21). Paul makes a distinction between those who "set their minds on earthly things" and those whose citizenship is "in heaven." Paul himself was a Roman citizen, who knew what privileges this brought – particularly on those occasions when he found himself in conflict with the Roman authorities. For Paul, Christians possessed something greater: the "citizenship of heaven," which is to be understood as a present possession, not something which is yet to come. While believers have yet to enter into the full possession of what this citizenship entails, they already possess that privilege. We have no permanent citizenship in this world, in that our citizenship is in heaven (Philippians 3:20). As the author of the Letter to the Hebrews puts it, "here we have no lasting city, but we are looking for the city that is to come" (Hebrews 13:14).

The Appearance of the Human Body in Heaven

The New Testament states that Christians are "citizens of heaven." But what do citizens of heaven look like? If heaven is to be compared to a human city, what are its inhabitants like? The New Testament has remarkably little to say about this, although it hints that such matters are a mystery, rather than known facts. The image of a seed, used by Paul in 1 Corinthians 15, was taken by many writers to mean that there was some organic connection between our earthly and heavenly bodies. Resurrection could thus be conceived as the unfolding of a predetermined pattern within the human organism. Yet even this image had to be treated with caution. While some theologians took the view that this obliged them to treat such matters with restraint, others appear to have seen themselves as liberated from the traditional constraints imposed by the biblical text, and launched into the most stratospheric of theological speculations.

One possibility would be to imagine the streets of the New Jerusalem as inhabited by disembodied souls. On this model, the human being consists of two entities: a physical body and a spiritual soul. Death leads to the liberation of the soul from its material body. This view was commonplace within the Greek-influenced culture of the New Testament period. However, it was vigorously opposed by most early Christian theologians. The most significant minority voice in this matter belonged to Origen, a highly creative theologian with a strongly Platonist bent, who held that the resurrection body was purely spiritual. This view was contested by most Christian writers, who insisted that the phrase "the resurrection of the body" was to be under-stood as the permanent resurrection of both the body and the soul of the believer.

But what would these resurrected individuals look like? Many early Christian writers argued that the "citizens of heaven" would be naked, recreating the situation in paradise. This time, however, nakedness would neither give rise to shame nor sexual lust, but would simply be accepted as the natural and innocent state of humanity. Others, however, argued that the inhabitants of the New Jerusalem would be clothed in finery, reflecting their status as citizens of God's chosen city.

It was clear to many writers that the final state of deceased believers was not of material importance to their appearance in heaven. The issue emerged as theologically significant during a persecution of Christians in the city of Lyons around the years

175–7. Aware that Christians professed belief in the "resurrection of the body," their pagan oppressors burned the bodies of the Christians they had just martyred, and threw their ashes in the River Rhone. This, they believed, would prevent the resurrection of these martyrs, in that there was now no body to be raised. Christian theologians responded by arguing that God was able to restore all that the body had lost through this process of destruction.

Methodius of Olympus (d. 311) offered an analogy for this process of reconstitution which would prove highly influential. He argued that the resurrection could be thought of as a kind of "rearrangement" of the constituent elements of humanity. It is like a statue which is melted down and reforged from the same material, yet in such a manner that any defects or damage are eliminated:

> It is as if some skilled craftsman had made a noble image, cast in gold or other material, which was beautifully proportioned in all its features. Then the craftsman suddenly notices that the image had been defaced by some envious person, who could not endure its beauty, and so decided to ruin it for the sake of the pointless pleasure of satisfying his jealousy. So the craftsman decides to recast this noble image. Now notice, most wise Aglaophon, that if he wants to ensure that this image, on which he has expended so much effort, care and work, will be totally free from any defect, he will be obliged to melt it down, and restore it to its former condition . . .
> Now it seems to me that God's plan was much the same as this human example. He saw that humanity, his most wonderful creation, had been corrupted by envy and treachery. Such was his love for humanity that he could not allow it to continue in this condition, remaining faulty and deficient to eternity. For this reason, God dissolved humanity once more into its original materials, so that it could be remodeled in such a way that all its defects could be eliminated and disappear. Now the melting down of a statue corresponds to the death and dissolution of the human body, and the remolding of the material to the resurrection after death.

A similar argument is found in the *Four Books of the Sentences*, the masterpiece of the great twelfth-century theologian Peter

Lombard. This book, which served as the core textbook for just about every medieval theologian, took the view that the resurrected body was basically a reconstituted humanity, from which all defects had been purged:

> Nothing of the substance of the flesh from which humanity is created will be lost; rather, the natural substance of the body will be reintegrated by the collection of all the particles that were previously dispersed. The bodies of the saints will thus rise without any defect, shining like the sun, all their deformities having being excised.

The twelfth-century Irish *Book of the Dun Cow* (Leabhar na Uidhre) so called because the vellum upon which it is written is supposedly taken from the hide of St. Ciaran's cow at Clonmacnoise – raises a further question concerning the nature of the resurrection body. What happens if the believer is *eaten*? The *Book of the Dun Cow* – presumably responding to genuine pastoral concerns at this point – argues that the various fragments of humanity, however scattered and variously decomposed they may be, are "recast into a more beautiful form" by the "fire of Doom." However, the work recognizes the importance of the precise place at which the believer dies:

> Those who have been devoured by wild animals and dispersed in various locations will arise according to the counsel of the Lord, who will gather them together and renew them . . . In this case, they will arise at the place at which they were devoured and dispersed, for this is what is reckoned to be their tomb.

A final question that has greatly vexed Christian theologians concerns the *age* of those who are resurrected. If someone dies at the age of 60, will they appear in the streets of the New Jerusalem as an old person? And if someone dies at the age of 10, will they appear as a child? This issue caused the spilling of much theological ink, especially during the Middle Ages. By the end of the thirteenth century, an emerging consensus can be discerned. As each person reaches their peak of perfection around the age of

30, they will be resurrected as they would have appeared at that time – even if they never lived to reach that age. Peter Lombard's discussion of the matter is typical: "A boy who dies immediately after being born will be resurrected in that form which he would have had if he had lived to the age of 30." The New Jerusalem will thus be populated by men and women as they would appear at the age of 30 (the age, of course, at which Christ was crucified) – but with every blemish removed.

The Beatific Vision: Seeing God Face to Face

The Christian hope is often expressed in terms of seeing the face of God directly, without the need for created intermediaries. In the Old Testament, divine favor is indicated by the face of God being turned towards an individual, just as disfavor is shown by that face being averted. In formal prayers or liturgies of this period, a worshipper might invoke God to "lift up [God's] countenance" (2 Kings 13:4; Isaiah 1:12; Ezekiel 32:11) as a means of securing the acceptance of the sacrifices or prayers being offered. If the face of God were "hidden" or "turned away," the believer had no hope of finding divine acceptance (Deuteronomy 31:17; Ezekiel 7:22).

Yet the image of the face of God concerns far more than the notion of the divine pleasure and favor. It also evokes the possibility of an encounter with the living God. To "see the face of God" is to have a privileged, intimate relationship with God – seeing God "as God actually is" (1 John 3:2), rather than having to know God indirectly, through images and shadows. Now we see God "as through a glass, darkly," but we shall finally see God face to face (1 Corinthians 13:12). The Book of Revelation affirms that this will be the privilege of those in heaven, where the saints will finally "see God's face" (Revelation 22:4).

This hope of seeing the face of God was developed extensively in the Christian tradition. In his *Letter 92*, Augustine of Hippo wrote to Italica, a noble widow, who had some questions concerning the hope of heaven. Augustine responded by fleshing out the brief biblical statements concerning "seeing God." While we are in exile on earth, we are not "fitted" or "adapted" to beholding the full glory of God; it is only when we ourselves are raised to glory and transformed that we may hope to see the radiance and glory of God in all their fullness:

> We see God according to the measure by which we are adapted to him . . . no matter how far we may advance, we still fall short of that perfection of likeness which is fitted for seeing God, as the apostle says, "face to face" . . . When you read, "Now we see through a glass darkly, but then face to face" (1 Corinthians 13:12), learn from this that we shall then see God face to face by the same means by which we now see him through a glass darkly. In both cases alike, the vision of God belongs to the inner person, whether while we walk in this pilgrimage still by faith, in which it uses the glass and the shadow, or when, in the country which is our home, we shall perceive by sight, a vision denoted by the words "face to face."

For Augustine, the vision of God possesses a unique capacity to satisfy human desire, utterly surpassing the ability of any created being or thing in this respect. Such a vision is the *summum bonum*, the supreme good, the "light by which truth is perceived, and the fountain from which all blessedness is drunk."

Augustine develops this idea further in the *City of God*, arguing that the vision of God in heaven sustains believers throughout their pilgrimage of faith:

> God himself, who is the Author of virtue, shall be our reward. As there is nothing greater or better than God himself, God has promised us himself. What else can be meant by his word through the prophet, "I will be your God, and you will be my people" than "I shall be their satisfaction, I shall be all that people honorably desire – life, health, nourishment, satisfaction, glory, honor, peace, and all good things"? This, too, is the right interpretation of the saying of the apostle "That God may be all in all." God shall be the end of all our desires, who will be seen without end, loved without cloy, and praised without weariness.

The nature of the vision of God enjoyed by the saints in heaven was the subject of no small debate throughout the Middle Ages. Pope John XXII provoked a particularly vigorous controversy through his argument that the saints who are now "under the altar" – a phrase deriving from Revelation 6:9 – are able to find consolation through contemplation of the humanity of Christ; after the resurrection and final judgment, however, they will finally be able to enjoy the full and perfect joy of seeing God directly. His successor Benedict XII tried to dampen down the somewhat heated exchanges which John provoked by arguing that those who were already purified were able to enjoy the vision of God before the end of time; others, however, would have to wait until history ended before the full revelation of the glory of God. But, he insisted, it would be worth waiting for.

Psalm 27:4 sets out the longing to see God in these words:

> One thing I ask of the Lord,
> This is what I seek;
> That I may dwell in the house of the Lord
> All the days of my life,
> To gaze upon the beauty of the Lord.

The Christian vision of heaven affirms that what the Psalmist longed for all his life will one day be the common privilege of the entire people of God: to gaze upon the face of their Lord and Savior, as they enter into his house, to dwell in peace for ever. It is no accident that Dante's *Divine Comedy* reaches its climax when the poet finally, after his epic journeys through hell and purgatory, emerges to behold "the love that moves the sun and the other stars."

Engaging with a Text

John Donne (1571–1631) is perhaps one of the greatest spiritual poets in the English language. The poem which follows is taken from the collection of "Divine Meditations," which deal with a range of theological and spiritual issues. The poem personifies Death and argues that it has been overthrown through the resurrection of Christ. It ends with the assertion of the final defeat and death of Death through the resurrection, which undergirds the Christian hope of heaven.

> Death be not proud, though some have called thee
> Mighty and dreadful, for thou art not so;
> For those whom thou think'st, thou dost overthrow,
> Die not, poor Death, nor yet canst thou kill me.
> From rest and sleep, which but thy pictures be,
> Much pleasure; then from thee, much more must flow,
> And soonest our best men with thee do go,
> Rest of their bones, and soul's delivery.
> Thou art slave to Fate, Chance, kings, and desperate men,
> And dost with poison, war, and sickness dwell,
> And poppy or charms can make us sleep as well
> And better than thy stroke; why swell'st thou then?
> One short sleep past, we wake eternally,
> And death shall be no more; Death, thou shalt die.

Donne's religious poetry is saturated with biblical themes, images, and ideas. It is important to bear in mind that the English translation of the Bible which Donne knew best is the great version commissioned by King James I in 1604, which was published in 1611. This is generally known as the King James Bible, although in England it is still often referred to as the Authorized Version. In what follows, we shall explore how biblical themes are incorporated into the poem.

1 Read the following verse from the King James version of the Bible:

The last enemy that shall be destroyed is death. (1 Corinthians 15:26)

How is this theme of death as an enemy incorporated into the poem? You might like to read the context in which this passage is set, and see how other images and ideas from this same source are worked into the poem. We shall consider another immediately.

2   Read the following verses from the King James Bible:

> Then shall be brought to pass the saying that is written, Death is swallowed up in victory. O death, where is thy sting? O grave, where is thy victory? The sting of death is sin; and the strength of sin is the law. But thanks be to God, which giveth us the victory through our Lord Jesus Christ. (1 Corinthians 15:55–7)

How is the theme of victory over death developed in the poem? In what way does Donne develop this idea? You might also like to reflect on the way in which this relates to those "theories of the atonement" which stress that Christ's death and resurrection are primarily to be understood as a victory over death, sin, and Satan.

3   Notice how Donne develops the idea of various analogies ("pictures") for death that we know from everyday life. Chief among them is sleep; what are the others? And how do you think Donne's use of analogies for death relate to the biblical and theological use of analogies for God?

4   Consider the following quotation from Donne:

> No man ever saw God and lived. And yet, I shall not live till I see God; and when I have seen him, I shall never die.

What idea does he express in this statement? How does it relate to the idea of the "beatific vision" we considered earlier in this chapter? And how does it relate to the poem you have just been reading?

Moving On

The aim of this introduction to the basics of Christian theology has been to encourage and stimulate you, by showing that you can explore some of theology's leading ideas and interact with some of its most important texts. It has also attempted to whet your appetite to know more, so that you will end this book feeling dissatisfied. This is all that a short book can hope to achieve when dealing with such a rich and complex subject.

In such a basic introduction to Christian theology, only a few theological topics can be examined. Many others need to be covered – including, for example, the doctrines of grace, human nature, the sacraments, and Christian understandings of the place of other religions. Questions of "theological method" have also been treated very superficially. For example, a much more extensive discussion of the sources and norms of theology is required.

In addition, hardly any historical contextualization has been provided. Both Martin Luther and John Calvin are introduced to readers; they are not, however, explained and examined in the light of the rise of the European Renaissance, and the origins of the Protestant Reformation. Thomas Aquinas is also introduced

– but there has not been enough space to explain how the movement known as "scholastic theology" developed, or to sketch its leading features. A much longer introductory text is required. This book represents a good start – but it is only a handshake to start a much longer conversation.

So where should you go next? Completing this book will be as far as some of you will wish to go in your theological explorations. But others will want to go much further. Perhaps you have chosen to read this book as an experiment – to see if there is any point in taking things further. If you were able to cope with this book, you will be able to handle the more extensive and comprehensive analysis in my more substantial work, *Christian Theology: An Introduction*. This shorter book was planned and written in such a way that it could lead into this much more thorough engagement with the history, ideas, and methods of Christian theology. You will find that your basic knowledge of theology will make this much more extensive encounter with this most fascinating discipline easier and more satisfying.

Christian Theology, now in its third edition, is designed to be used in a variety of contexts, including individual private study, taught courses, and group study. It has become the field-specific bestseller in the English-speaking academic and seminary communities, and has been translated into nine languages. Its three major sections provide an overview of the history of Christian theology, its sources and methods, and its fundamental ideas. If you want to know more, this is the place to go.

You may also find the accompanying volume *The Christian Theology Reader* useful. This contains more than three hundred readings, each with its own individual introduction, commentary, and study questions. If you felt encouraged by the engagements with theological texts offered in every chapter of this basic introduction, you will be able to handle and benefit from the much more extensive coverage of this larger work.

However, some of you will choose to end your studies here. If so, I would like to thank you for allowing me to accompany you on your exploration of theology, and wish you well in the future. Perhaps I might quote from Karl Barth in bidding you farewell at this point, and encourage you to see theology as something that is helpful for the individual life of faith, as well as for the life and witness of the church:

> Theology is not a private subject for theologians only. Nor is it a private subject for professors. Fortunately, there have always been pastors who have understood more about theology than most professors. Nor is theology a private subject of study for pastors. Fortunately, there have repeatedly been congregation members, and often whole congregations, who have pursued theology energetically while their pastors were theological infants or barbarians. Theology is a matter for the Church.

Brief Glossary of Theological Terms

What follows are brief definitions of some of the technical terms used in this book or which arise from it.

adoptionism The heretical view that Jesus was "adopted" as the Son of God at some point during his ministry (usually his baptism), as opposed to the orthodox teaching that Jesus was Son of God by nature from the moment of his conception.

Anabaptism A term derived from the Greek word for "rebaptizer" and used to refer to the radical wing of the sixteenth-century Reformation, based on thinkers such as Menno Simons and Balthasar Hubmaier.

analogy of faith (*analogia fidei*) The theory, especially associated with Karl Barth, which holds that any correspondence between the created order and God is only established on the basis of the self-revelation of God.

analogy of being (*analogia entis*) The theory, especially associated with Thomas Aquinas, that there exists a correspondence or analogy between the created order and God, as a result of the divine creatorship. The idea gives theoretical justification to the practice of drawing conclusions about God from the known objects and relationships of the natural order.

ancilla theologiae   A Latin phrase meaning "handmaid of theology," used to refer to the practice of using philosophical or cultural ideas as a helpmate or dialogue partner for Christian theology.

apostolic era   The period of the Christian church, regarded as definitive by many, bounded by the resurrection of Jesus Christ (ca. AD 35) and the death of the last apostle (ca. AD 90?). The ideas and practices of this period were widely regarded as authoritative, at least in some sense or to some degree, in many church circles.

appropriation   A term relating to the doctrine of the Trinity, which affirms that while all three persons of the Trinity are active in all the outward actions of the Trinity, it is appropriate to think of those actions as being the particular work of one of the persons. Thus, it is appropriate to think of creation as the work of the Father, or redemption as the work of the Son, despite the fact that all three persons are present and active in both these works.

Arianism   A major early Christological heresy, which treated Jesus Christ as the supreme of God's creatures and denied his divine status. The Arian controversy was of major importance in the development of Christology during the fourth century.

atonement   An English term originally coined in 1526 by William Tyndale to translate the Latin term *reconciliatio*, which has since come to have the developed meaning of "the work of Christ" or "the benefits of Christ gained for believers by his death and resurrection."

Barthian   An adjective used to describe the theological outlook of the Swiss theologian Karl Barth (1886–1968), and noted chiefly for its emphasis upon the priority of revelation and its focus upon Jesus Christ. The terms "neo-Orthodoxy" and "dialectical theology" are also used in this connection.

Beatific Vision A term used (especially in Roman Catholic theology) to refer to the full vision of God, which is allowed only to the elect after death. However, some writers, including Thomas Aquinas, taught that certain favored individuals – such as Moses and Paul – were allowed this vision in the present life.

Calvinism An ambiguous term, used with two quite distinct meanings. First, it refers to the religious ideas of religious bodies (such as the Reformed church) and individuals (such as Theodore Beza) who were profoundly influenced by John Calvin, or by documents written by him. Second, it refers to the religious ideas of John Calvin himself. Although the first sense is by far the more common, there is a growing recognition that the term is misleading.

Cappadocian Fathers A term used to refer collectively to three major Greek-speaking writers of the patristic period: Basil of Caesarea, Gregory of Nazianzus, and Gregory of Nyssa, all of whom date from the late fourth century. "Cappadocia" designates an area in Asia Minor (modern-day Turkey) in which these writers were based.

Cartesianism The philosophical outlook associated with René Descartes (1596–1650), particularly in relation to its emphasis on the separation of the knower from the known, and its insistence that the existence of the individual thinking self is the proper starting point for philosophical reflection.

catechism A popular manual of Christian doctrine, usually in the form of question and answer, intended for religious instruction.

Catholic An adjective which is used both to refer to the universality of the church in space and time, and also to a particular church body (sometimes also known as the Roman Catholic church) which lays emphasis upon this point.

Chalcedonian definition The formal declaration at the Council of Chalcedon that Jesus Christ was to be regarded as having two natures, one human and one divine.

charisma, charismatic   A set of terms especially associated with the gifts of the Holy Spirit. In medieval theology, the term "charisma" is used to designate a spiritual gift, conferred upon individuals by the grace of God. Since the early twentieth century, the term "charismatic" has come to refer to styles of theology and worship which place particular emphasis upon the immediate presence and experience of the Holy Spirit.

Christology   The section of Christian theology dealing with the identity of Jesus Christ, particularly the question of the relation of his human and divine natures.

consubstantial   A Latin term, deriving from the Greek term *homoousios*, literally meaning "of the same substance." The term is used to affirm the full divinity of Jesus Christ, particularly in opposition to Arianism.

creed   A formal definition or summary of the Christian faith, held in common by all Christians. The most important are those generally known as the Apostles' Creed and the Nicene Creed.

deism   A term used to refer to the views of a group of English writers, especially during the seventeenth century, the rationalism of which anticipated many of the ideas of the Enlightenment. It is often used to refer to a view of God which recognizes the divine creatorship, yet which rejects the notion of a continuing divine involvement with the world.

Docetism   An early Christological heresy, which treated Jesus Christ as a purely divine being who only had the "appearance" of being human.

Donatism   A movement, centering upon Roman North Africa in the fourth century, which placed a strong emphasis on the need for personal holiness on the part of church members and their ministers, and on the need for measures to enforce this where necessary.

Ebionitism   An early Christological heresy, which treated Jesus Christ as a purely human figure, although recognizing that he was endowed with particular charismatic gifts which distinguished him from other humans.

ecclesiology   The section of Christian theology dealing with the theory of the church.

Enlightenment, the   A term used since the nineteenth century to refer to the emphasis upon human reason and autonomy, characteristic of much of Western European and North American thought during the eighteenth century.

eschatology   The section of Christian theology dealing with the "end things," especially the ideas of resurrection, hell, and eternal life.

eucharist   The term (used in this book) to refer to the sacrament also variously known as "the mass," "the Lord's Supper," and "holy communion."

exegesis   The science of textual interpretation, usually referring specifically to the Bible. The term "biblical exegesis" basically means "the process of interpreting the Bible." The specific techniques employed in the exegesis of scripture are usually referred to as "hermeneutics."

exemplarism   A particular approach to the atonement, which stresses the moral or religious example set to believers by Jesus Christ.

Five Ways, the   A standard term for the five "arguments for the existence of God" associated with Thomas Aquinas.

Homoousion   A Greek term, literally meaning "of the same substance," which came to be used extensively during the fourth century to designate the mainline Christological belief that Jesus Christ was "of the same substance of God." The term was polemical, directed against the Arian view that Christ was "of similar substance (*homoiousios*)" to God. See also **consubstantial**.

Incarnation   term used to refer to the assumption of human nature by God, in the person of Jesus Christ. The term "incarnationalism" is often used to refer to theological approaches which lay especial emphasis upon God becoming human.

logos   A Greek term meaning "word," which played a crucial role in the development of patristic Christology. Jesus Christ was recognized as the "word of God"; the question concerned the implications of this recognition, and especially the way in which the divine "logos" in Jesus Christ related to his human nature.

modalism   trinitarian heresy, which treats the three persons of the Trinity as different "modes" of the Godhead. A typical modalist approach is to regard God as active as Father in creation, as Son in redemption, and as Spirit in sanctification.

monophysitism   The doctrine that there is only one nature in Christ, which is divine (from the Greek words *monos*, "only one," and *physis*, "nature"). This view differed from the orthodox view, upheld by the Council of Chalcedon (451), that Christ had two natures, one divine and one human.

orthodoxy   A term used in a number of senses, of which the following are the most important: orthodoxy in the sense of "right belief," as opposed to heresy; Orthodoxy in the sense of the forms of Christianity which are dominant in Russia and Greece; orthodoxy in the sense of a movement within Protestantism, especially in the late sixteenth and early seventeenth centuries, which laid emphasis upon need for doctrinal definition.

parousia   A Greek term, which literally means "coming" or "arrival," used to refer to the second coming of Christ. The notion of the *parousia* is an important aspect of Christian understandings of the "last things."

patristic   An adjective used to refer to the first centuries in the history of the church, following the writing of the New Testament (the "patristic period"), or thinkers writing during this period (the "patristic writers"). For many writers, the period thus designated seems to be ca. 100–451 (in other words, the period between the completion of the last of the New Testament writings and the landmark Council of Chalcedon).

Pelagianism   An understanding of how humans are able to merit their salvation, diametrically opposed to that of Augustine of Hippo, placing considerable emphasis upon the role of human works and playing down the idea of divine grace.

perichoresis   A term relating to the doctrine of the Trinity, often also referred to by the Latin term *circumincessio*. The basic notion is that all three persons of the Trinity mutually share in the life of the others, so that none is isolated or detached from the actions of the others.

Radical Reformation   A term used with increasing frequency to refer to the Anabaptist movement – in other words, the wing of the Reformation which went beyond what Luther and Zwingli envisaged, particularly in relation to the doctrine of the church.

Reformed   A term used to refer to a tradition of theology which draws inspiration from the writings of John Calvin (1510–64) and his successors. The term is now generally used in preference to "Calvinist."

schism   A deliberate break with the unity of the church, condemned vigorously by influential writers of the early church, such as Cyprian and Augustine.

scholasticism   A particular approach to Christian theology, associated especially with the Middle Ages, which lays emphasis upon the rational justification and systematic presentation of Christian theology.

soteriology   The section of Christian theology dealing with the doctrine of salvation (Greek: *soteria*).

transubstantiation   The doctrine according to which the bread and the wine are transformed into the body and blood of Christ in the eucharist, while retaining their outward appearance.

Trinity   The distinctively Christian doctrine of God, which reflects the complexity of the Christian experience of God. The doctrine is usually summarized in maxims such as "three persons, one God."

two natures, doctrine of   A term generally used to refer to the doctrine of the two natures, human and divine, of Jesus Christ. Related terms include "Chalcedonian definition" and "hypostatic union."

Details of Theologians Cited

Abelard   *see* Peter Abelard.

Anselm of Canterbury (ca. 1033–1109)   Born in Italy, Anselm migrated to Normandy in 1059, entering the famous monastery of Bec, becoming its prior in 1063, and abbot in 1078. In 1093 he was appointed archbishop of Canterbury. He is chiefly noted for his strong defense of the intellectual foundations of Christianity, and is especially associated with the "ontological argument" for the existence of God

Aquinas   *see* Thomas Aquinas.

Arius (ca. 250–ca. 336)   The originator of Arianism, a form of Christology which refused to concede the full divinity of Christ. Little is known of his life, and little has survived of his writings. With the exception of a letter to Eusebius of Nicomedia, his views are known mainly through the writings of his opponents.

Athanasius (ca. 296–373)   One of the most significant defenders of orthodox Christology during the period of the Arian controversy. Elected as bishop of Alexandria in 328, he was forced to resign on account of his opposition to Arianism. Although he was widely supported in the West, his views were finally recognized after his death at the Council of Constantinople (381).

Augustine of Hippo (354–430) Widely regarded as the most influential Latin patristic writer, Augustine was converted to Christianity at the Northern Italian city of Milan in the summer of 386. He returned to North Africa, and was made bishop of Hippo in 395. He was involved in two major controversies: the Donatist controversy over the church and sacraments, and the Pelagian controversy over grace and sin. He also made substantial contributions to the development of the doctrine of the Trinity, and the Christian understanding of history.

Barth, Karl (1886–1968) Widely regarded as the most important Protestant theologian of the twentieth century. Barth moved away from liberal Protestantism during World War I, and adopted a theological position which placed an emphasis on the priority of divine revelation. His early emphasis on the "otherness" of God in his Romans commentary (1919) was continued and modified in his monumental *Church Dogmatics*. Barth's contribution to modern Christian theology has been immense.

Basil of Caesarea (ca. 330–79) Also known as "Basil the Great," this fourth-century writer was based in the region of Cappadocia, in modern Turkey. He is particularly remembered for his writings on the Trinity, especially the distinctive role of the Holy Spirit. He was elected bishop of Caesarea in 370.

Bonhoeffer, Dietrich (1906–45) A German Lutheran theologian, influenced by Karl Barth, with a particular interest in ecumenical work during the 1930s. He was arrested in 1943 and hanged by the Nazis in 1945. His letters and papers from prison include significant discussions of the suffering of God, and the need for theology to relate to a "religionless society."

Brunner, Emil (1889–1966) A Swiss theologian who, while being influenced by his fellow countryman Karl Barth, developed ideas on natural theology which distanced them during the later 1930s. He is particularly noted for his strongly personalist idea of revelation.

Bultmann, Rudolf (1884–1976) A German Lutheran writer, who was appointed to a chair of theology at Marburg in 1921. He is chiefly noted for his program of "demythologization" of the New Testament, and his use of existential ideas in the exposition of the twentieth-century meaning of the gospel.

Calvin, John (1509–64) A leading Protestant reformer, especially associated with the city of Geneva. His *Institutes of the Christian Religion* has become one of the most influential works of Protestant theology.

Cyprian of Carthage (d. 258) A Roman rhetorician of considerable skill who was converted to Christianity around 246, and elected bishop of the North African city of Carthage in 248. He was martyred in that city in 258. His writings focus particularly on the unity of the church, and the role of its bishops in maintaining orthodoxy and order.

Descartes, René (1596–1650) French philosopher noted for his emphasis on the role of systematic doubt, and the importance of "perfection" in discussion of the nature of God.

Edwards, Jonathan (1703–58) A leading American theologian in the Reformed tradition, noted especially for his metaphysical defense of Christianity in the light of the increasingly influential ideas of the Enlightenment, and his positive statements of traditional Reformed doctrines.

Gregory of Nazianzus (329–89) Also known as "Gregory Nazianzen." He is particularly remembered for his "Five Theological Orations" written around 380, and a compilation of extracts from the writings of Origen, which he entitled the *Philokalia*.

Gregory of Nyssa (ca. 330–ca. 395) A leading Cappadocian Father, with a special interest in the relation of Christian theology and Platonic philosophy.

Gregory the Great (ca. 540–604) Also known as Gregory I. He was elected as pope in 590 and did much to establish the political power of the papacy, which reached its zenith in the Middle Ages. As a theologian, he is particularly noted for his pastoral and exegetical works.

Hugh of St. Victor (d. 1142)   A theologian of Flemish or German origin, who entered the Augustinian monastery of St. Victor in Paris around 1115. His most important work is *de sacramentis Christianae fidei* ("On the Sacraments of the Christian Faith"), which shows awareness of the new theological debates which were beginning to develop at this time.

Ignatius of Antioch (ca. 35–ca. 107)   A major early Christian martyr, noted for his letters to Christian churches in Asia Minor. Of particular interest is his vigorous defense of the reality of Christ's human nature and sufferings, in the face of those who wished to maintain that they were simply an appearance.

Irenaeus of Lyons (ca. 130–ca. 200)   Probably a native of Asia Minor, who was elected as bishop of the Southern French city of Lyons around 178. He is chiefly noted for his major writing *adversus haereses* ("Against the heresies"), which defended the Christian faith against Gnostic misrepresentations and criticisms.

Jenson, Robert (b. 1930)   North America's leading Lutheran theologian, noted for his major contributions to the doctrine of the Trinity.

Julian of Norwich (ca. 1342–ca. 1415)   Little is known of the life of this English mystic, apart from the details she herself provides in her *Sixteen Revelations of Divine Love*. For at least part of her active life, she lived as a solitary in the city of Norwich.

Justin Martyr (ca. 100–ca. 165)   One of the most noted of the Christian apologists of the second century, with a concern to demonstrate the moral and intellectual credibility of Christianity in a pagan world. His *First Apology* stresses the manner in which Christianity brings to fulfillment the insights of classical philosophy.

Lombard, Peter   *see* Peter Lombard.

Luther, Martin (1483–1546)   Perhaps the greatest figure in the European Reformation, noted particularly for his doctrine of justification by faith alone, and his strongly Christocentric understanding of revelation. His "theology of the cross" has aroused much interest in the late twentieth century. Luther's famous Ninety-Five Theses on Indulgences (October 1517) are generally regarded as marking the beginning of the Reformation.

Melanchthon, Philip (1497–1560) A noted early Lutheran theologian, and close personal associate of Martin Luther. He was responsible for the systematization of early Lutheran theology, particularly through his *Loci Communes* (first edition published in 1521) and his "Apology for the Augsburg Confession."

Methodius of Olympus (d. ca. 311) A noted critic of Origen's theology, particularly the doctrines of the transmigration of souls and a purely spiritual resurrection body. His treatise on the resurrection develops the thesis of the continuity between the pre- and post-resurrection bodies.

Origen (ca. 185–ca. 254) Leading representative of the Alexandrian school of theology, especially noted for his allegorical exposition of scripture, and his use of Platonic ideas in theology, particularly Christology. The originals of many of his works, which were written in Greek, have been lost, with the result that some are known only in Latin translations of questionable reliability.

Paley, William (1734–1805) A leading English exponent of natural theology and the argument from design.

Pascal, Blaise (1623–62) An influential French Roman Catholic writer, who gained a considerable reputation as a mathematician and theologian. After a religious conversion experience in 1646, he developed an approach to his faith which was strongly Christocentric and experiential. His most famous writing is the collection known as the *Pensées*, first gathered together in 1670, some years after his death.

Peter Abelard (1079–1142) French theologian, who achieved a considerable reputation as a teacher at the University of Paris. Among his many contributions to the development of medieval theology, his most noted is his emphasis upon the subjective aspects of the atonement.

Peter Lombard (ca. 1100–60)   A noted medieval theologian, active at the University of Paris, who was appointed bishop of Paris in 1159. His most significant achievement was the compilation of the textbook known as the "Four Books of the Sentences," a collection of extracts from patristic writers.

Rahner, Karl (1904–84)   One of the most influential of modern Roman Catholic theologians, whose *Theological Investigations* pioneered the use of the essay as a tool of theological construction and exploration.

Sayers, Dorothy L. (1893–1957)   English novelist and dramatist, with a strong interest in Christian theology.

Tertullian (ca. 160–ca. 225)   A major figure in early Latin theology, who produced a series of significant controversial and apologetic writings. He is particularly noted for his ability to coin new Latin terms to translate the emerging theological vocabulary of the Greek-speaking Eastern church.

Thomas Aquinas (ca. 1225–74)   Probably the most famous and influential theologian of the Middle Ages. Born in Italy, he achieved his fame through his teaching and writing at the University of Paris and other Northern universities. His fame rests chiefly on his *Summa Theologiae*, composed towards the end of his life and not totally finished at the time of his death. However, he also wrote many other significant works, particularly the *Summa contra Gentiles*, which represents a major statement of the rationality of the Christian faith.

Thomas à Kempis (ca. 1380–1471)   A leading representative of the *Devotio Moderna*, who is widely accepted to be the author of the classic work of spirituality known as the *Imitatio Christi* ("The Imitation of Christ").

Tillich, Paul (1886–1965)   A German Lutheran theologian who was forced to leave Germany during the Nazi period, and settled in the United States. He held teaching positions at Union Theological Seminary, New York, Harvard Divinity

School, and the University of Chicago. His most significant theological writing is the three-volume *Systematic Theology* (1951–64).

Vincent of Lérins (died before 450)   A French theologian who settled on the island of Lérins. He is particularly noted for his emphasis on the role of tradition in guarding against innovations in the doctrine of the church, and is credited with the formulation of the so-called "Vincentian canon."

Wesley, Charles (1707–88)   An English writer of hymns and a theologian, noted for his Pietist emphases and hostility to Calvinism. Along with his brother John, he contributed to a significant revival within eighteenth-century English Christianity.

Wesley, John (1703–91)   An English theologian, pastor, and hymn-writer, remembered especially as the founder of Methodism. Like his brother Charles, he was deeply influenced by Pietism, which had a considerable impact on his early theology. His theology found its expression in hymns and sermons, rather than works of systematic theology.

Zinzendorf, Nicolas Ludwig von (1700–60)   A German writer who reacted against the rationalism of the theology of his day, and emphasized the emotional and experiential aspects of Christian faith. There is a clear connection between Zinzendorf's ideas and those of Pietism. He is remembered especially as the founder of a religious community at Herrnhut.

Zwingli, Huldrych (1484–1531)   Also known as Ulrich Zwingli. A leading Swiss reformer, particularly associated with the vigorous denial of the real presence of Christ at the eucharist, a view usually designated "Zwinglianism." He died in battle, as a result of his attempts to spread his reforming ideas in his native Switzerland.

Index